DROPPING OUT
Issues and Answers

ABOUT THE AUTHORS

James A. Farmer, Ph.D., is assistant professor of social work at
The University of Texas at Arlington, School of Social Work, a
consultant to human service agencies and has a part-time private
practice. Prior to his teaching position, he worked as a social worker
with aggressive adolescents, led parenting groups and counseled
substance abusers. His involvement with youth began in 1969 when
he worked in a boy's club in Joliet, Illinois. Later, while pursuing
graduate degrees at the University of Iowa and Ohio State University,
he developed workshops for youth and parents focusing on communication in parent-teen relationships. Dr. Farmer has written exten-
sively in the area of adolescent behavior. He is the author of two
books entitled, *Positive Influence: A Practice Guide for Dealing with
Teenage Aggression* and *High-Risk Teenagers: Real Cases and Intercep-
tion Strategies with Resistant Adolescents.*

Yolanda Payne, Ph.D., received her Master's degree from Teacher
College, Columbia University and a doctorate at University of
Illinois in Education Psychology. Dr. Payne has been a university
professor at Southwest Missouri State University and has worked as
education consultant for City College of New York. She was a state
program evaluator at the State of Louisiana (evaluated a number of
education programs). Dr. Payne has worked also with alternative
education and dropout prevention programs in Illinois and Florida.
Currently she is an adjunct professor at Georgia State University.

DROPPING OUT

Issues and Answers

By

JAMES A. FARMER, PH.D.

and

YOLANDA PAYNE, PH.D.

CHARLES C THOMAS • PUBLISHER
Springfield • Illinois • U.S.A.

Published and Distributed Throughout the World by

CHARLES C THOMAS • PUBLISHER
2600 South First Street
Springfield, Illinois 62794-9265

© *1992 by* CHARLES C THOMAS • PUBLISHER

ISBN 0-398-05812-1

Library of Congress Catalog Card Number: 92-14838

With THOMAS BOOKS *careful attention is given to all details of manufacturing
and design. It is the Publisher's desire to present books that are satisfactory as to their
physical qualities and artistic possibilities and appropriate for their particular use.*
THOMAS BOOKS *will be true to those laws of quality that assure a good name
and good will.*

Printed in the United States of America
SC-R-3

Library of Congress Cataloging-in-Publication Data

Farmer, James A., 1950–
    Dropping out : issues and answers / by James A. Farmer and Yolanda
Payne.
        p.   cm.
    Includes bibliographical references (p.   ) and index.
    ISBN 0-398-05812-1 : $16.95
    1. Dropouts—United States.   2. Education—United States—Aims and
objectives.   I. Payne, Yolanda.   II. Title.
LC143.F37   1992
373.12′913′0973—dc20
                                                                                                    92-14838
                                                                                                    CIP

PREFACE

Dropping Out: Issues and Answers attempts to identify and address issues relevant to the problem of the "dropout." It is not enough to present statistics regarding the incidence of dropouts or to present information about dropout prevention efforts. Issues involving the dropout must be identified and addressed before we can expect to alleviate the problem of the dropout in America. *Dropping Out: Issues and Answers* attempts to do that.

The problem of the dropout is more than youth leaving school before graduation. Rather, the problem is that as our society changes and becomes a more technological one it will be impossible for the dropout to blend into the larger social order. There are few, if any, jobs for these youth. Youth who drop out create problems not only for themselves but for society also.

This book has attempted to identify issues surrounding the dropout and to answer questions often asked by youth who are considering leaving school. Questions often asked include, "Why should I stay in school?" "What is the purpose of school?" and "What is school doing for me?" This book may be used as a supplemental textbook in a foundation of education course. It will prove informing to those who are questioning the present concern regarding the dropout and dropout prevention efforts.

This book was written for parents, educators, social service workers, and the general public. It is also recommended reading for individuals who have dropped out of school, students in dropout prevention programs or students who are questioning school and why they must attend school.

Chapter 1, *Introduction,* is an overview of the book with emphasis upon describing the problem.

Chapter 2, *Youth Who Drop Out,* describes the consequences to the youth who drops out of school. The chapter presents an overview of what the youth who drops out of school can expect. It presents case studies

v

which focus upon youth who have dropped out and youth who are at risk of dropping out.

Chapter 3, *Identification of Potential Dropouts,* presents and discusses specific warning signs that parents, teachers, and friends should be aware of which will help them to identify students who are at risk of dropping out.

Chapter 4, *School—A Necessary Tool of Socialization,* examines the purpose of school and required school attendance. Formal education is presented as a necessary tool of education which prepares the individual to function independently within the larger social order and to contribute to that social order. Students should be made aware of the purpose or why of school. The question is often asked, "Are schools preparing youth to function in our technological society?"

Chapter 5, *The Relevance of School,* looks at the relevance of our schools for today.

Chapter 6, *The Dropout—What Are the Reforms?* compares formal education today with formal education in the past.

Chapter 7, *Preventing Student Dropout,* looks at what is being done to keep students in school.

Chapter 8, *What Now, Making School Appealing to the Youth of Today,* looks at school in the 1990s and what should be done to make school more appealing to the youth of today.

Chapter 9, *Pulling It All Together,* discusses conclusions and implications of this book.

ACKNOWLEDGMENTS

The journey from idea to print has been a long one and many have helped us along the way. Thanks and acknowledgments go to all who inspired and energized us. Dr. Theresa Bey was helpful in reading the manuscript and offering suggestions. Dr. Mitchell Rice, Dr. Paul Kim and Ira Tolbert were supportive in the completion of the manuscript. Judy Linville and Jo Ann Stevenson helped in the typing. Dr. Pedro Lecca and Dr. Shirley King provided us with encouragement. Drs. Roy and Jackie Jacobs helped along the way and kept us motivated.

Most of all we thank Virgil, Isaac, Tremaine, James, Jr., Jerome and Kenya, for tolerating our frequent absences from them while we worked on this book. Without their love and support our undertaking such a project could never have succeeded.

CONTENTS

DROPPING OUT
Issues and Answers

Chapter One

INTRODUCTION

A high school diploma is certification that an individual has met the minimum requirements for full participation in American society. It is the minimum requirement for many non-professional jobs. For example, the armed services requires that its enlistees possess a high school diploma. It is impossible to obtain decent employment without it.

Twenty years ago it was assumed by parents, employers and school personnel that everyone would complete high school. However, students often dropped out of high school due to the need to help support the family. The family needed the extra income provided by the youth. After dropping out of high school, a youth often in future years bemoaned the fate which followed a dropout.

An alarm is being sounded by educators, parents and the media. Children and youth are failing to complete a high school education or a GED. Florida has defined a dropout as "a student who leaves school for any reason except death before graduation or completion of a program and without transferring to another public or private school or other educational institution" (Florida Statutes, Section 228.4). Approximately 30 percent of our nation's students entering high school will drop out prior to graduation. Here are a few questions of major concern to parents, educator and professional helpers. Will the increase in dropouts adversely affect the nation and its economy? What happens to individuals who drop out? The answer is, we can no longer afford an increasing number of students leaving high school before completing a program of study. Some of the negative consequences are:

a. Higher susceptibility to unemployment
b. Lower earnings
c. Increased crime
d. More welfare clients
e. Increased number of illiterates
f. High rate of unwed mothers

Higher Susceptibility to Unemployment

The U.S. Department of Labor statistics have shown that the lower the educational achievement, the more the likelihood of a person becoming unemployed. Moreover, poverty and unemployment seem to be reflected in educational level, income and number of children. Studies have estimated a loss of around $200,000 in lifetime earnings for a male high school student who fails to graduate or complete a GED.

School dropouts are more likely to end up on welfare, homeless and/or incarcerated. A high percentage of juvenile and adult inmates are former high school dropouts. The welfare client, the homeless and ex-convict are more likely to be unemployed.

Female teenagers who drop out of school are more likely to end up on welfare. A strong probability exists that when teen-age parents are eligible for welfare benefits, many of them will become dependent on public programs such as Aid to Families With Dependent Children (AFDC), food stamps and Medicaid. Welfare clients tend to have difficulty in securing employment, and some of them quickly settle into a welfare lifestyle.

Lower Earnings

Educational level is directly related to employee earning power. If an individual is a high school dropout, he/she will probably receive lower earnings. It is common to see higher incomes among the more educated. Lower jobs are directed to the less educated and the less likely to advance.

The other side of the coin is that we (society) will always have a large pool of lower earning individuals. Certain jobs do not require high educational attainment. For example, bus boys, cooks, janitors and dish washers will continue to be needed in the community. The school dropout fits into these roles with little if any adjustment problems. The counter argument is, however, that our society is becoming high tech and informational. Where once we were accustomed to seeing employees doing physical labor, we are seeing them replaced with high technology. During the past ten years, our society has witnessed a growth in the area of robotics and specialized computers. High tech systems will challenge the teenager who drops out of school in the 1990s.

Increased Crime

Numerous studies have shown we are experiencing an increase in crime. Some key indicators are socioeconomic level, the youth's educational status, and early academic performance. Students who do not enjoy school will eventually quit unless something dramatically changes their attitude. When a youth quits school, there is a possibility he/she will turn to crime. Crime becomes an alternative when the youth is unable to locate employment.

More Welfare Clients

Dropouts are over-represented in the welfare line. Adolescents with poor academic skills who become young mothers and fathers are more likely to become welfare clients than those who stay in school. It is estimated that 6 billion dollars may be spent on teenage pregnancy. Many teenage parents will end up on Medicaid, Aid to Families With Dependent Children (AFDC) and food stamps. A poverty lifestyle tends to cause some teenage parents to become dependent on public programs.

Increased Number of Illiterates

It should be noted that some students who drop out of high school may be borderline illiterate. A major factor and one of the best predictors of a potential dropout is poor academic performance. It is not uncommon to see dropouts who cannot fill out applications or read instructions. Moreover, some have not learned to speak standard English. Poor oral skills may hinder a youth from climbing socially. For example, not long ago, a young man approached me about his English speaking ability. While on his job he noticed that a number of new hirees were promoted over him. He was told by a vice president of the company that he was not ready for an upward move when he inquired about promotion. Later that day John went home feeling somewhat angry. He spoke with his wife, and she suggested that he talk with other employees about his lack of job mobility. During a discussion, one of his co-workers pointed out that John needed to clean up his poor English. John was surprised. As far as he was concerned, he spoke standard English. For the first time, he began to realize that he communicated on a non-standard English level. John wondered, could this be the reason why he has not been promoted?

John purchased a miniature tape recorder, and over a three day period he recorded everything that he said. Later he took his tape recorder to an English teacher and asked her to critique his grammar. John was told that he spoke non-standard English. The next day when he saw the vice president with whom he had talked earlier, John mentioned that he was taking lessons in communication. The vice president's eyes lit up. He explained that the company would pay for the classes, and John might get the next promotion.

John was held back because of poor language skills. Many youth who did not complete high school, and were poor English students, experience similar problems. Nonstandard English can prevent job promotions.

High Rate of Unwed Mothers

More and more teenagers are getting pregnant and having babies. Unfortunately, some of these girls believe if love cannot be found within their family, an alternative is to have a child who will love them as a parent.

Another cause of teen pregnancy is the lack of knowledge of sexual intercourse and contraceptives. Teenagers explore their sexual desires and do not fully understand love, sex and relationships. Because of their confusion, many of them enter into unhealthy relationships. For instance, the other day I received a telephone call from a nineteen year old female. This young lady asked me, "How do you know when you are in love?" She had been living with an unmarried man. She cared about him, but she viewed him as boring. She explained, "He is nice and buys me everything, but I don't love him. Why can't I love him? Last year I had a miscarriage. I lost his baby. And he wants me to have another baby."

This example is typical. Some young females end up "living" with a guy and become confused about the relationship. The young woman was a high school dropout and had not been given the opportunity to explore relationships with various males. Instead, she immediately began living with a male whom she didn't know if she wanted to marry. Chances are she will get pregnant again and have a baby for him.

THE RELEVANCE OF A HIGH SCHOOL EDUCATION FOR TODAY'S YOUTH

Is formal education and the obtaining of a high school diploma valued as it was twenty years ago? The answer is no. At one time formal education was envied by those who did not possess it. Formal education was often perceived as the right of the wealthy and the upper class. Education was something to be valued because of the knowledge it presented to the individual. For some, knowledge was desired and valued. An education was an end and not a means to an end. Our government developed the public schools, eventually mandated that all youngsters should attend school until they had completed their high school education or reached the age of sixteen. The public schools were modeled upon private schools. The desire was to provide the student with a well-rounded education similar to that of the individual who went to private schools. What has happened? Because of television, radio, newspapers and books, knowledge has become more accessible to the masses. Some youth reason they don't need to go to school in order to learn about the world around them. Many youth have been educated in their day-to-day interactions with other people. Gradually, formal education has come to represent getting a good paying job. In fact, some youth are motivated to stay in school so that they may obtain a better paying job.

Are young people convinced of the value of a high school education? As I reflect over my school days, I must acknowledge that I stayed in school and completed high school because it was expected of me. The thought of not completing high school never entered my mind. I didn't know I had a choice. None of my peers dropped out of school.

After completing high school, I continued my studies because it was expected of me. It was only later I began to understand that the completion of high school was a "rite of passage" into adulthood. I was fortunate, but what about the individual who drops out of school before earning his or her high school diploma?

Jerry

Jerry was a high school dropout, who believed he did not need a high school diploma. He viewed his chances of getting and maintaining employment to be as good as the next guy. From his perspective, high school was a waste of time.

Jerry believed he was intelligent and highly motivated. These were the only two ingredients a young man needed to succeed in life. When filling out an application at the employment office, he was confident he would be employed. Over a course of six months, Jerry never received any call to come for an interview or to come to work. He became disappointed when he learned that many of his friends who had graduated from high school were working at "good" jobs. After a year of no employment, Jerry became depressed. To manage his problem of depression, Jerry began drinking and sharing drugs with his friends. He spent seven days a week consuming drugs and alcohol. His parents became outraged at his behavior and often threatened to throw him out of the house.

A year later, Jerry was offered employment. He would be earning $12 an hour and receive two weeks' vacation. Although Jerry was very happy about his new job, another problem had arisen. Because Jerry had become a consumer of large quantities of drugs and alcohol, he had developed a substance addiction. He was a substance abuser, and it took a large sum of money to support his habit. He spent his paycheck on drugs and alcohol. As an outgrowth of his substance abuse, Jerry's personal drug problem grew worse. He was fired for selling drugs on the job.

This example highlights a young man who may have had a wonderful future had he not dropped out of school. When opportunity finally arrived, Jerry was "strung out" on drugs and alcohol. The addiction was too overpowering for Jerry to stay employed. Someone like Jerry usually ends up in prison or dead over a drug deal.

I am familiar with a young girl who completed high school. When asked if she was disappointed in her high school education, she replied, "No. Completing high school was learning within itself," she said. Because she finished high school, her earning power increased. With our emphasis upon monetary rewards, should future earning power be the only incentive for completing a program of study? I say no, because a youngster often fails to think about money and the buying power of money until he/she is placed in the situation where he/she is forced to provide his/her own housing, food, clothes and living expenses. A job paying $6 an hour appears excellent when mom and dad are paying the rent and buying the food. Often mom and dad continue to buy clothes for a youngster long after he/she has left school. Teenagers don't realize that in order to become an adult they must be able to function independently of parents. From my observations, I have seen young people who could not fill out an employment application without assistance.

A few years ago, I was approached by a young man who appeared very confused. I had earlier observed him going into the personnel office. They were unable to help him. He approached me. Unable to help him, I took him to the information desk and returned to my office. Later, I observed, Mary, the lady at the information desk, helping him complete an application. He wanted to apply for a job. She went over each question on the application with him and told him what to write. At times she became agitated with his misunderstanding but was very patient with him. I am under the impression Mary had probably helped young people in this situation on more than one occasion.

Completing high school teaches the individual skills necessary to effectively function in society. My grandparents could not read very well. It was not as important then as it is today. Our culture will no longer tolerate illiteracy.

SCHOOL, A TOOL OF SOCIALIZATION

We are in a period of great change and upheaval in the world. This period of dramatic change in the world is not the time for increased dropouts within American society. The dropout often becomes a burden to society. Rather than having an increased rate of dropouts, the nation needs youth who pursue advanced education. We lose so much when youths drop out of school. Leaving school is more than a matter of decreased earning power. It is also a matter of unfinished or incomplete socialization. Socialization is the process of preparing the individual to assume a role within a social group.

Learning and participation in school activities has a particular meaning. Studying American history is more than learning meaningless factors. It instills pride and respect for our country.

Formal education is indeed a socialization process and the individual who does not complete this process fails to complete his/her socialization as prescribed by our government. Well-informed citizens are a necessity to any society. John F. Kennedy said it so well, "Ask not what your country can do for you but rather ask, what you can do for your country." The best way to bring down a society or a group is to attack and destroy its youth. To destroy their motivation is to impede their socialization.

Forbid their education and subsequent learning of their history and eventually that social group will falter.

REASONS FOR LEAVING SCHOOL

There are many reasons for leaving school. Some of the most cited causes are dislike of school, low academic achievement and a desire to work. Smith (1986) determined that students with positive attitudes toward school and teachers were least likely to drop out of school for school-related reasons. Wehhlage and Rutter (1985) noted that in the typical high school where there are many dropouts, teachers are not particularly interested in students; the discipline system is perceived as neither effective nor fair. Students who start off skipping school are in danger of dropping out. Research has indicated that some students drop out of school because of behaviors which occurred earlier in their lives, particularly between the ages of 11 and 15. Some students drop out of school because of bad experiences with teachers and peers. Students who do poorly in school or fall behind their classmates have a higher probability of dropping out of school.

In summary, school dropouts cite a variety of reasons for leaving school. Educators and professional helpers need to establish early intervention techniques to curb this problem. If we are to have an impact on the increasing rate of school dropouts, we must begin now.

PREVENTING STUDENT DROPOUT: WHAT IS BEING DONE?

There are many dropout prevention programs that are helpful to students. Some are:

Cities in School

Cities in School is a private non-profit program that is effective with school districts. This dropout prevention program includes a class where participants discuss such topics as careers, drug abuse and teen pregnancy. It also features frequent visits by local business leaders. This program offers counseling, tutoring, incentives and home visits. However, Cities in School has been criticized for its system of tracking students. The program tracks only students enrolled in the program but does not track them once they leave the program.

Tutoring by College Students Campus Compact

Campus Compact, an organization of 203 colleges and universities across the country is pushing the tutoring program. This service is comprised of volunteer college students who tutor underachievers and students at risk.

Alternative Schools

Alternative schools provide a humanistic approach to dropout prevention programs. Students are given individualized attention and academic support. Efforts are directed at helping participants to receive a GED, employment and/or vocational training.

Burger King Academics

Burger King Academics help youth in academics, social problems and job-hunting. Youth receive academic instructions, and employment in a Burger King restaurant. They learn to work in a fast food setting. As a result, some of them are promoted to a position of manager or assistant manager.

Dropout prevention efforts provide a range of services. Are such programs successful? In some instances they are. It depends on how success is defined. Success, for some, may mean any program willing to enroll a youth into activities and provide supportive counseling when problems arise. To others, success may be defined by the number of youth the program is able to keep off the juvenile court roll. Regardless of the definition of success, dropout prevention programs serve a purpose and many of them are doing a good job.

Chapter Two

YOUTH WHO DROP OUT

A youth at risk presents many problems to our society. They are a problem to the school district in various ways. For example, you may remember the commercial which says, "A mind is a terrible thing to waste." When teens drop out of school, we lose a valuable product. These individuals might have become leaders in our communities and society. Jesse Jackson, who was reared by his mother, grew up to be nominated for President of the United States. Les Brown, who was labeled and placed in the "Opportunity" special education class, grew up and became a state legislator and finally a motivational speaker who speaks to Fortune 500 corporate executives. When a teen drops out, chances are he or she may turn to illegal means of surviving.

We have heard of the youth who sells drugs for $5000 a day profit, rides in a new car and lives the life of the rich and famous. This person has learned how to obtain the American dream the wrong way. Illegal opportunities afford some youth a means of satisfying their appetite. When youth doesn't have the skills or education to get a "good paying job," they will have a difficult time delaying what they perceive will gratify their appetite. Do cars, luxury apartments and gold rings satisfy their desire? It partially satisfies their craving, but a more important point is that material objects are a symbol of success. The American Dream is being successful at whatever you do and showing others you have achieved it. Youth have learned this principle and are not afraid to try alternative routes to success even if they must turn to illegal activities. Young people see success symbols everywhere. For example, Tarzan fought African tribe people, conquered wild animals and won the love of Jane, his success symbol. Clarence Thomas had to pay a terrible price, but he still achieved his success symbol, to become a Supreme Court justice. Young people also pay a price. Many of them want to be successful. They have acquired their personal success symbols. It doesn't matter whether we agree or disagree with their chosen success symbol, because the point is that they have selected what they believe to be their symbol of success. Here are a few examples.

Bob

Bob is age 18, has two sons by two women and is in the twelfth grade. He has two part time jobs and attends Belmont High School. Bob was a fair athlete who used to dream of getting a sports scholarship and enrolling in a nearby college. However, he began running into financial difficulties and getting pressure applied regarding child support. To relieve some of the pressure, Bob began jogging and spending more time at home. He believed exercise would reduce his personal stress. At one point he began to feel better because of exercising, but he still had to deal with the fact he was broke.

Bob began drinking and smoking "pot" with his newly acquired friends. He didn't know them, but they seemed to be okay. They always had plenty of booze, pot and girls for everybody. Six months into the relationship with his friends, Bob was introduced, by Sam, to cocaine. At first Bob hesitated because he remembered all the negative advertising he had heard about drugs. He wanted to "just say no" to the drugs, but his life had become complex. Bob had pressures from poor grades, paying child support, and drugs. Bob grabbed his head and screamed, "I just need a break." Every day he consumed cocaine while school became secondary. He lied, cheated and stole to get money for cocaine. Eventually this drug was the only reason why he lived.

He dropped out of school and later was caught robbing a store in his neighborhood. Bob went to prison for five years. After prison he returned to his home town, married and found a job, but once again was dissatisfied in his financial situation. Bob later became a drug dealer so that he could buy a new car and increase his bank account. The drugs gave Bob a profit of $5000 a day. He acquired not only a new car and a large bank account, he bought a $300,000 home, jewelry, and all the things that go with a luxury life style.

Bob wanted to become a success in our society. Like so many young males, Bob valued the American Dream but fell short of reaching it the legitimate way. When success symbols drive people, short cuts and dangerous strategies will be found to achieve success. A prison term did not detour Bob from reaching his goal. Tunnel vision and immediate gratification are two driving forces that keep many young people striving.

Betty

Betty is age 17, an eleventh grader with no children. Her father is a college professor, and her mother is a school teacher. Betty enjoys school and receives high grades. Her best subjects are math, English and psychology. Betty says she wants a career as a psychologist with a private practice.

Betty has had an isolated or sheltered upbringing. Her parents have tried to shield her from the poisonous elements in our society. For example, Betty was not allowed to date because her parents who are traditional, wanted total control over Betty's life. As an outgrowth of this behavior, Betty began to take risks. She enjoyed planning and working out detailed schemes on how to slip guys into her bedroom at night. Sometimes she would invite several guys to have sex all night. Betty started to fantasize about promoting sexual activity with several of the male school teachers. Within a brief time, Betty controlled several of her male teachers who taught various courses to her. When students turned in homework assignments, Betty did not. When tests were given, Betty never studied but received an "A." If Betty wanted to be excused from class, she was never questioned.

Betty was invited to become a student representative to a local politician's organization. Her parents and the school were very proud of her. This was a great honor and a major step into the political arena. After three months, Betty had become sexually involved with local politicians and she was quickly moving up the ladder to the mayor. Betty finally lost interest in school and dropped out. There were many reasons for this. She became pregnant and did not know the name of the father. Another reason is that when they found out about her sexual encounters, her parents disowned her.

Several months later, Betty became a prostitute and enjoyed this life style. She was not afraid of AIDS and was willing to take her chances. As long as she was having sex, she was happy. Did she complete her education? No, she never completed it because she believed she was making as much money as a bank executive, and loving her work more.

There are many young people who fall between the cracks. They continue on the wrong track never getting better but only becoming worse. Betty is an example of that. How many Bettys are there in various communities who turn to prostitution, drugs and crime? If Betty could have been helped, she might have become an engineer, physician, lawyer or a psychologist. I wonder what career her child will enter? Parents influence their children's hopes, desires and dreams. Will Betty's child become the psychologist of which Betty once dreamed, or will the child enter prostitution?

Jack

Jack is age 16, a Hispanic adolescent. Several months ago, he was released from Eldora Juvenile Correctional Institute where he served two years. Inside the correctional program, Jack met many boys who were doing time. Most of the boys felt they were innocent and got a raw deal from the juvenile court judge. Many of them became good friends with Jack and taught him how to survive inside the correctional system. Jack learned what to say and what not to say to custody workers. He learned how to con correctional staff. When he was participating in psychotherapy, he learned how to say everything the treatment staff wanted to hear. Jack became proficient in talking about feelings and relating feelings to his parents. Since the treatment team was deep into the psychodynamic model, Jack listened to his comrades explain the basic principles and then they roleplayed Jack's performance. Jack had to work hard at showing tears in group session. The therapist would not believe he was conning if he ever cried. The boys spent hours talking about how to lie and cheat at games. Jack also learned how to steal cars, break into homes and rob stores. There were moments that Jack believed he was inside a school of crime. These boys had learned their trade well and were highly skilled. Jack was learning so rapidly he didn't have time to absorb his academics. As an outgrowth of this, his academics were low but his criminal marks were high.

Finally Jack was released from Eldora Juvenile Correctional Institute. Jack was a happy boy. He had made friends and learned a variety of trades. Not only had he learned how to cook, but he acquired skills in criminal activity. Jack returned to his home town and enrolled in Drake High School.

The teachers at Drake High School were a little fearful of Jack. They had heard all sorts of hearsay and did not know what to believe. Some heard he carried a gun on his waist and a knife near his ankle. Others had heard tall tales about Jack. One tall tale was that Jack killed a boy and the police never found out it was Jack who killed him. Because of the lies and hearsay circulating around school, Jack was a little nervous about what students and teachers had heard. He felt insecure about his academic performance and insecure about his identity as a student. His parents wanted him to get a job since both of them were high school dropouts and currently were assigned a probation officer. Like his parents, Jack had to report to a probation officer once a week. Jack didn't mind the probation officer, but he would have liked someone of the same race. Jack perceived white probation officers having a prejudicial attitude.

About one-third of the way into the school term, Jack began to have problems academically and socially. His academic performance was low, and students alienated themselves from Jack. As a result of this, Jack's attitude started to slowly change. He realized he was a person with a whole set of values different from his classmates. He had been locked up for two years and now it was time to apply what he had learned. Jack dropped out of school and began hanging around the wrong juveniles. They drank beer, alcohol and consumed drugs. Drugs were easy for Jack to get, because everyone wanted him to have them. It was not long before Jack was busted and returned to the correctional institute. However, because of his age and prior history of illegal activity, Jack went to the adult correctional system.

In summary, Jack never made it in the School System. Like many low-income kids he was labelled as a social misfit or anti-social. Jack turned to crime because this was all he had learned at Eldora. He wanted to change but he did not have the social skills and motivation to do this alone. There are a lot of Jacks who fall between the cracks and never make it.

Chapter Three

IDENTIFICATION OF POTENTIAL DROPOUTS

Public schools are not educating all of our teenagers. Some are at-risk students. An at-risk student is viewed by some school personnel as a potential dropout or trouble maker. At-risk children and youths are becoming an increasing problem for educators, parents and professional helpers. One of the major reasons this problem still exists is because of our presumable fashion used to identify at-risk children and youth. What are the characteristics which place some students in danger of not completing their high school education? Traditional methods of assessing a child and determining at-risk behavior have involved:

1. Test Performance.
   Low scores on standardized tests.
2. Records.
   Prior arrest record.
   Prior school record.
   Prior psychiatric consultation.
3. School—classroom behavior.
   Behavioral disorders.
   Reaction toward teacher, principal and student peers.
4. Community Services.
   Juvenile Justice System.
   Mental Health Counseling.

TEST PERFORMANCE

One of the major reasons students drop out of school is low test scores. Teachers, school counselors, social workers and principals have access to student test scores. In many cases, students are stereotyped by the score they received on a standardized test. If youths received a low score, they may be seen as students with low performance and little opportunity for a college education. It is not uncommon to read stories such as the following:

19

Jack, 33, is a Ph.D. and a psychologist for the Veteran's Administration in Washington D.C. He graduated from high school with a "D" average. Jack was told by his school counselor to forget about a college education. He was advised to get a factory job and become a solid American who pays taxes. On the contrary, Jack desired a college degree.

He worked in a factory about one year and because of frustration, gave up his job. His goal was to obtain a college degree and not work his life away as a factory worker.

Jack enrolled in a community college and received an Associate of Arts degree. He later enrolled in a small college and obtained a degree in psychology with a grade point average of 3.40. After three years of working in a hospital, Jack applied for admissions into a graduate program in psychology. Upon completion of his masters degree, Jack was strongly encouraged by the head of the psychology department to enter a doctoral program in psychology at Ohio State University. Jack was admitted and obtained a Ph.D. in counseling psychology.

Jack's story is not unusual. Jack's grades were low; some thought he showed little promise of succeeding academically. His counselor and teachers stereotyped him. They failed to perceive Jack's motivation and determination to succeed. Test scores are only one indicator of academic performance. Some school personnel view test scores as the only indicator of educational success. Jack proved that one could succeed in spite of low test scores.

Records

Students' records follow them. Negative and positive information are written about students. After a student has been incarcerated or has an arrest record, this will show up in his/her file. Teachers refer to student records to get a general idea of what type of student they are teaching. The school record is important in intervention strategy because it allows school personnel to develop a student profile. On the other hand, school records can be a negative label and become a brand. Once a youth has been labeled a troublemaker it is difficult to remove this tag.

School-Classroom Behavior

Class disruptions occur in schools. When teachers, principals and student peers react negatively to unwanted behavior disruptions, school personnel will look for strategies to remove the student from class. Behavior disorders will get school personnel's attention quickly.

Community Services

The Juvenile Justice System does its share in creating barriers and labels for young people. Research reveals that lower class black youth often become "prime" candidates for the Juvenile Justice System while many middle class white youth receive mental health counseling services. This may be due to our legal system which often views race as a contributing factor to juvenile delinquency. Often after going through the Juvenile Justice System, a youth is labeled. This label may be referred to as a brand. In the school system, the youth may be branded as a misfit. After having been incarcerated for over a year, he/she may experience difficulty making the transition from a juvenile institution to a public school system.

There is a growing awareness of children and youth who are in need of services, but knowledge of support services in the area of at-risk students is often less than successful in meeting the needs of youth. Some of the problems identified as causing at-risk behavior are:

Dislike of School

Some schools are impersonal. Some teachers tend to favor certain students more than others. Students who give a correct answer are often called upon more than those who are unprepared. Teachers draw closer to students who appear to enjoy school and their teachers. Personal variables also play an important role in whom the teacher likes and dislikes.

When students do not like their teachers, they will not value the course work. Many may complain that their homework is too hard and too much. They perceive teachers and principals as having a deaf ear to their needs. The school has few rewards for a student who doesn't want to be part of the system.

When a youth does not like school, some school personnel may develop an insensitive interpersonal style in their interaction with the youth. These are the youths who are eventually pushed out of our schools first. When this happens, school dropouts turn to drugs, crime and prostitution, and some may become part of the teen-age homeless. Many cannot read or write and they are blocked from social mobility. Some of them become our unemployed, illiterate and welfare recipients.

Low Academic Achievement

At-risk children and youths have low academic achievement. Some are passed from one grade to the next. These students were removed from certain teachers' classrooms, because they lacked motivation and had poor grade performance. Passing students carries the problem to another grade level. Letting children pass as long as they are not a behavior problem is creating illiterates in society.

A Desire to Find Employment

When students are not finding success in school, they may turn to outside employment. Since educational rewards for potential dropouts are minimal, these students will search for alternative means for self-gratification. Whether a job is part-time or full-time, employment and self-gratification become the student's immediate method of improving self-esteem.

It is not uncommon to hear juveniles describing their reaction to school: "Learning history is not going to get me a job. What I need is a job to buy a new car." When youth realize they are unlikely to receive school gratification, they often turn away from academic learning. There is a major concern for "feeling good." Youth desire to experience everything that will make them feel good—fast cars, drugs, sex and money.

The home situation becomes more turbulent because parents are resistant to a youth's decision to leave school. This means youth must find employment to support themselves. Without the family financial support, it becomes difficult to survive independently of the family.

Our streets are crowded with homeless dropouts. Others are incarcerated. Some juvenile institutions and adult prisons are filled with individuals who are lacking early home structure and discipline. Many juveniles find structure and discipline in juvenile institutions. Inside the institution, juveniles are told what to do and when to do it. Teenagers need structure in their life.

DRUG USAGE

Each local school system strives to prevent and stop drug usage. Are we winning the "war on drugs" in schools? Yes, we are. Positive gains occur at almost every grade level. Local school systems are providing greater flexibility in reaching out to youth. Public schools provide in-service training for school personnel, teachers and school counselors. The schools also provide awareness workshops and programs that motivate students to say "no" to drugs.

Although adults perceive drugs as the culprit, juveniles view drugs differently. When the school system rejects young people, drugs offer an alternative. This alternative is bleak, yet to the teenager who is alone, drugs are an option. The danger of drugs is overlooked and the thrills and pleasures are emphasized. Immediate gratification becomes a major theme. The notion, "I want what I want when I want it," is given priority. When youth want an instant high, they might steal drugs to acquire the high. They will do whatever it takes to maintain a constant high. School is secondary in an at-risk youth's life. Education is more or less associated with a negative experience. Drugs allow teenagers to "feel good" and provide them with a false sense of joy.

FAMILY-SCHOOL RELATIONS

Sometimes parents are the last ones to discover their son/daughter has not been attending school. While many parents believe large numbers of youth dislike school, few believe their son/daughter will turn up on the dropout roll. When this occurs, parents blame the school system for being unresponsive to the needs of their son/daughter. A clear indicator of a parent's success with school personnel is how the parent perceives the attitude of individual school personnel. Parents look for school personnel to be warm, open and direct with them. When they see school personnel as defensive, indirect, lying and evasive, parents become suspicious. A suspicious parent is an enemy of teachers and principals. Here is an example of a parent who perceives the school as an enemy:

Ms. Fisher received numerous telephone calls about her son. Dale had been admitted into an alternative school and was displaying behavioral problems, according to the social worker. Dale claimed the principal and teachers physically assaulted him. On several occasions, Dale said a teacher grabbed his throat. When Ms. Fisher heard Dale's story she immediately went to the school and demanded to see the principal. She was told that the principal could not be disturbed. Ms. Fisher pounded on the counter and yelled, "Where is that mutha fucker who beats children." The principal walked out of his meeting and tried to calm Ms. Fisher. At that point, Ms. Fisher verbally assaulted the principal.

That evening Ms. Fisher hid outside of the school and watched the principal and teacher through binoculars. She was very suspicious of the school. However, Ms. Fisher never found any evidence of child abuse.

A week later there was another school conference about Dale's behavior. We invited his parents to attend. Ms. Fisher declined; however, Mr. Fisher accepted. During the conference, Mr. Fisher pulled out a 12 inch knife and began picking his fingernails with the blade point. As the psychologist talked about Dale's behavior problems, Mr. Fisher stated:

> When I tell Dale to do something, he does it. We don't have problems with him at home. He obeys me. When I give him a chore, he completes it. Dale never talks back to me. I don't understand why the school is having problems with my son. Can you tell me why we see a good boy at home and you see a bad boy at school?

Dale is a manipulator. He plays the role of perfect little boy in the home and at school he is a behavioral problem because he threatens teachers and physically assaults students. Dale has fooled his parents by the "nice boy" routine he plays in the home. His parents have not seen the devilish side of his personality because he controls his behavior when he is with them. He manipulates his environment to achieve his objective.

PREGNANCY

Teen pregnancy is common among young girls. An unwanted pregnancy can cause a girl to drop out of school. Some years ago, when a girl became pregnant it was an embarrassment to the girl, the boy and the parents. Now it is common and the same embarrassment spoken about earlier is not present today. In fact, some females see teen pregnancy as an alternative. Elvira, a high school student, told her school counselor the following:

Counselor: Elvira, have you prepared for a career?

Elvira: I haven't had time.

Counselor: Do you plan to prepare for a career?

Elvira: I don't need a career.

Counselor: What do you mean?

Elvira: Well, when I get out of school I plan to get on welfare.

Counselor: Welfare! You don't have any children. What about a career and marriage?

Elvira: I don't need a man. I want a child whom I can love and care for.

Counselor: You have too much potential to get on the welfare roll. You can work, get a job.

Elvira: I don't want a job. I can't depend on a job. I can count on the welfare system. My mother is on welfare and her mother was on welfare. They did all right.

Counselor: I am shocked that you would think like this.

Elvira: I am not the only person who believes this way. Many girls don't want to marry or attend college. It is tough to get a job without a degree or some kind of training. I don't need a degree or training to get on welfare. My mother has four children and receives welfare benefits. She doesn't have a high school diploma.

Counselor: But you can find a nice young man to marry and have a family. Your husband will take care of you. Or, you can enroll into a vocational tech program. You must try to improve yourself. Welfare is not the way to go.

Elvira: I don't want a man living with me. I have girlfriends who have two and three children. The fathers of those children do not work or contribute to the welfare of the children. The father will wait until the girl is on welfare and then show up to eat and frequently ask to borrow money. I don't want a man living with me. There aren't any good men around. Many of them are on drugs and want you to support their habit.

Some teens perceive welfare as an alternative lifestyle. And, more and more teens are turning to welfare. I am convinced that education should prepare students for the employment market and motivate them to stay off welfare rolls. No teenager should desire to receive welfare benefits as an option to employment.

PERSONALITY AND ADJUSTMENT PROBLEMS

Counselor: Why were you sent to the office?
Student: I punched Billy in the nose.
Counselor: What made you act out like this?
Student: He called me a liar.
Counselor: Couldn't you have found another way of dealing with your differences?
Student: No, he got what he deserves.

This is a brief excerpt from the files of many school counselors and social workers. From the student's point of view, the problem has been dealt with. However, students are not allowed to strike out at other students when there is a negative transaction. The student in the above excerpt would say, "I've worked out the problem and selected the best alternative to resolve this conflict." The problem is that we cannot have students displaying physical aggression toward another youth. So the student probably would be suspended from school. At this point, the solution could resolve the problem, but it doesn't. If a youth believes he/she has been treated unfairly by the school, the youth may see this personal experience as an assault on his/her self-esteem. The fact that the school has responded by suspension doesn't change the reality that Billy is a liar.

Unmotivated

It's difficult to get motivated when one feels the entire school is against you. To be branded a troublemaker or potential school failure is a tough burden to bear. Teachers will look for any excuse to turn over a trouble-maker to the office. It makes me wonder who is really the culprit—the teacher or the student.

A student's motivation drops when he/she realizes that the school has a deaf ear. It does not take a genius to figure out who is on the teacher's black list. The notion that "some teachers are out to get you" sometimes scares a youth into striking back.

Another reason why some juveniles are unmotivated is because of learning disabilities. No one wants to feel dumb and stupid among his/her classmates. The embarrassment of consistently receiving low grades produces social pressure and tension. Anger turned toward self and acting out are common ways of releasing tension. In many cases, when a youth presents himself/herself as a behavioral problem, this will hide the real problem—learning disability.

FAMILY PROBLEMS

Most experts believe that a disrupted family life may cause juveniles to drop out of school. However, the relationship between family problems and a high dropout rate is ambiguous. Some of the contributing factors are: (1) broken homes, (2) lack of parental involvement, (3) peer group, (4) financial problems, and (5) incarceration.

Broken Homes

Children need a close relationship with family members in order to prevent delinquency. Research efforts have consistently supported the relationship of family closeness and delinquency prevention. Children who wander the streets and consistently are involved with the juvenile justice system display high levels of insensitivity, detachment, manipulation and more distance from family members.

Practitioners claim that the parents' method of providing warmth, closeness and support is probably directly related to their children's level of warmth, closeness and supportive behavior. There is significant evidence that teenagers will role model their parents' behavior. Looking at this relationship another way, youth who believe that their parents are providing them with parental involvement are more likely to imitate their parents' child rearing involvement. Cold and detached parents beget cold and detached children.

Lack of Parental Involvement

Uncaring parents cut across racial, ethnic, religious and socioeconomic backgrounds, affecting the entire spectrum of society. Such parents cannot be categorized by age, sex, or educational level. They represent all walks of life, with varying cultural and economic backgrounds.

Uncaring parents have unrealistic perceptions of the stages of child development. When their children are acting up or are inappropriate, these parents may react out of control. Parents such as these are a bomb walking around looking to explode. When the child does something small but inappropriate, the parent blows up and files away the incident as another black mark against the child.

Unstable parents who are unable to cope with stressful events eventually burn out. As a result of this, parents withdraw their physical attachment and some even withdraw affection. Other parents become angry and throw away their kids.

Peer Group

Youth groups meet an unmet need in a young person. Teenagers may join a gang to receive recognition from peer members, when recognition has been missing from his/her psychological development. It is logical to conclude that a youth may find a group of youngsters to satisfy an unmet need.

Financial Problems

Parents who excessively complain about financial woes keep family members under pressure. These parents often have a "short fuse" and may be more critical of their children. They may be less tolerant of their children's inappropriate behaviors. Financial problems may send parents into a "worry wart" syndrome. When finances are low even though the cost of raising children is skyrocketing, parents who are not "making ends meet" may explode over the most minor incidences. Teenagers who are the target of these explosions often do not understand fully the pressures placed on their parents. Some teenagers view their parents as unfair and overly controlling.

As stated earlier, unstable parents are often unable to cope with stress. Similarly these parents may be unfair and overly controlling in their attempt to cope with financial burdens. This is a problem because when teenagers are pushed too far, many will retaliate. Kids may fight back by displaying low school performance and behavior disorders. They perceive their parents as too critical and overly demanding.

Incarceration

During my tenure as a social worker in an adolescent program, I encountered several teenagers who were incarcerated for one year. After their release, these youth returned to our program. In regard to their educational level, these youth lost a year of schooling and their school performance dropped. Their attention span was short and we experienced more behavioral problems from them. Their teacher's attitudes were often negative, and the other youth saw them as outsiders or potential troublemakers.

It is tough making the transition back into the classroom after a juvenile has been incarcerated. Juveniles who have been incarcerated are sensitive and notice other's reaction to them. When objects are stolen from school or homes broken into, in many instances these juveniles are the first ones questioned. It is often difficult for a youth "to get back on the right track" after being incarcerated. Some choose to drop out of school and get a job rather than stay in school and be seen as a "bad seed."

In summary, the identification of potential dropouts is not an easy task. We have attempted to point out factors associated with the increasing number of school dropouts. Our school system must make a commitment toward helping potential dropouts if they want to make a difference. The increasing number of dropouts is not the problem of the school system only. Parents must become more aware of their behavior and its effect upon their youth. Community support programs are needed for youth prior to their leaving school.

Chapter Four

SCHOOL—A NECESSARY
TOOL OF SOCIALIZATION

Every society, regardless of how primitive it is, develops standards for its members. Those who expect to function within the society must be willing to abide by the norms of the society. The history of our nation is filled with the success stories of men who amassed fortunes without having completed school. Society's norms have changed. At one time in our national history schools were primarily for the wealthy. It was automatically assumed that children of the wealthy would be sent to school while the children of the poor received little if any formal schooling. This changed with the development of our public education system. Next we developed compulsory attendance laws which required that all children must attend school until the age of sixteen. We then saw the development of the secondary school. It was later determined that we needed some method to certify that an individual had completed the requirements of the secondary school. This led to the high school diploma. Initially there was little if any negative status attached to having not earned a high school diploma. This has gradually changed.

Until recently individuals could easily obtain employment without having earned their high school diploma. This is no longer the case. One of the many questions one is asked on a job application is "what high school did you attend and what year did you graduate"? The completion of secondary school is now expected within our society. The tool (school) has been developed which will prepare all future citizens for their prospective role within the larger society.

To not complete high school or to drop out of high school before earning a diploma is to discontinue the process of certification that one is capable of functioning within the larger society. Some may ask, what about the youngster who says, "Look I don't want to waste my time in high school taking boring classes. I know what I want to do with my life and I feel that I should be allowed to do it." Does this individual have the freedom to make such a statement without negative consequences? Individuals had the opportunity to make such a statement during the early years of our school system, but that is no longer the case. The individual who chooses this option is labeled a dropout. He/she soon discovers that many opportunities are closed to him/her. If he/she attempts to enlist in the armed services he/she will discover that a high school diploma is required. When he/she attempts to obtain gainful employment, he/she will discover that he/she can only acquire menial jobs which pay a minimum wage, if that. Often these individuals are forced to go back to school to obtain a graduate equivalent degree. The youngster failed to understand the role of school in the process of socialization. He/she failed to realize that school is more than just a place where he/she goes and sits each day. He/she failed to grasp the purpose of school. This failure may have been the catalyst that lead to his/her eventually becoming bored and dropping out of school. The essence of the matter is that we must abide by the norms of our society if we expect to be functioning members of society. Relevant or not, individuals are expected to attend a secondary school and to acquire a certificate which indicates that they have completed the requirements of that school (high school diploma). What can be done? The first thing is to make students aware of the purpose of school as soon as possible.

THE PURPOSE OF GOING TO SCHOOL

My son recently began school. He is now in the second grade. He has homework which must be completed, thus he can no longer just play or sit and watch television. Learning to read is exciting to him. He sometimes sits and reads to me. We have worked out a system in which he pronounces the words that he knows when reading, and I pronounce the words he is unable to pronounce. My husband and I attempt to buy books for him that are challenging but not intimidating. Now, however, the initial excitement of school and homework has passed. He has come to resent homework, although he continues to enjoy school. Often he does not give us his homework because he knows that we will make him do it. He often asks why must he do homework. Our response is to explain to him how doing his homework helps him. Because my son loves to read, I often explain to him that doing his home work will help him to learn more words and therefore increase his reading skills. Although only seven years old, my son wants to know how school and completing homework is going to benefit him. He wants to know, "Why am I doing these things?" It is not enough to simply tell him you are doing these things because you must do them or because I want you to do them. I must admit that initially it was sometimes difficult explaining to my son why he must go to school and why he must do his homework. Children at that age do not see a purpose to school. It was difficult until I realized that I must help him to understand how school benefits him. My response to his questions about the why of his participation in school activities was the initial foundation upon which is built his school successes and failures. Many adults view participation in school as something that must be done. Some of them resented school when they attended it, and these attitudes are often transmitted to their children. These adults have never stopped to ponder the why of school.

The Pledge of Allegiance was one of the first things I learned when I began school. Each day as part of our devotion we were required to say the pledge of allegiance to the flag. Of course we all memorized it. It was only later that I realized that this builds patriotism and love of country. Students continue to say the Pledge of Allegiance to the flag as part of their morning devotion. I recently worked at a high school at a dropout prevention program and an in-house suspension program. I was pleasingly surprised when I discovered that high school students were required to recite the Pledge of Allegiance to the flag each morning. Some argue that the main purpose of school is to cultivate the individual's mind. A question I must ask is "To cultivate the individual's mind to do what?" Sure we want individuals to be stimulated and to reach their maximum potential, but most of all we want them to move into the larger society and to perpetuate that society. School prepares them for this move. If we are honest we must admit that in many instances we want the individual to think a certain way and to see life in a certain way. In fact we may punish the individual who refuses to think and act in the prescribed manner.

The age old questions about the why of school have come down through the generations. I am sure that the majority of the readers when entering school wondered why they had to go to school. I wondered why I had to sit all day and do the things I did at school. I was given no explanation. Maybe some of my peers would have enjoyed school more if school had been made an exciting adventure to them and if they were shown the purposes of school. Some may say that a child is unable to understand these things but I disagree. A child needs meaning and purpose in his/her life just as an adult needs meaning and purpose.

One of my students shared her experiences with her son and how she used his interest in and love of art as a catalyst for improved work in mathematics. I will attempt to allow her to tell it in her own words. We will call her Mary.

> My son did not like math and put forth little effort in it. He would not do his math homework. He loved to draw and wanted to spend all of his spare time drawing. He indicated to me that he wanted to be an architect. That was all I needed to hear. I began to explain to him about the role of mathematics for the architect. I stressed to him that he would need to be competent in mathematics in order to be an architect. His desire to be an architect served as a motivation for his improved effort in mathematics. I realize now that I gave him a reason to strive to do his best in math. I showed him how mathematics would benefit him. It is no longer something he has to do. Math has become something that he wants to do."

The Why of School

School is a means to an end. It is not an end in itself. Gutek, (1988, p. 4) noted that "as a special learning environment, staffed by specialists in education, the school is designed to educate by providing the young with a structured and organized access to the culture's tools, skills, knowledge and values." Let's examine his statement a little more closely. Why must the young be made aware of their culture's tools, skills, knowledge and values? They must be made aware of these things if they are going to function in that culture and become contributing members of that culture. Beck (1965) noted that school is often viewed from a utilitarian perspective. I must admit I am one who views school from a utilitarian perspective. I perceive school as first and foremost a tool of socialization. The main goal or purpose of school is to prepare the student to assume a role within the larger social order. The emphasis in our schools is upon preparing the student to survive in our society, and to survive the challenges of our society. Stop and think about it. Why do most parents send their children to school? Ask any parent why do they send their children to school and they will probably respond that they want them to be able to get a good job and support themselves. A common expression often made by parents is, "I want my children to learn all they need to know in order to get a good job." From my own experiences I now realize that there are some things that children are going to need to know if they are going to survive in our social order. Some may ask, "What does school do?" School prepares the individual for life by introducing him/her to and teaching him/her things he/she needs to know if he/she is to become a functioning member of our society.

Preparation for Life

Complaints are often made about the so-called "how-to" courses that are the "supposedly" subject matter of our schools, but I find no reason to complain. If I were to complain, my complaint would be that we fail to introduce students to the opportunities and challenges that await them upon the completion of school, although this is sometimes done for special groups who are identified as at risk of dropping out of school in an effort to motivate them to stay in school. Why not do this for all children regardless of their achievement? Why not begin this process at approximately the third grade? As an example, my husband is an assistant professor of chemistry at a local university. He and a number of his students often perform magic shows for local high school students. They perform a number of chemical experiments with results which appear to be magic for the watching students. The students love it. The goal is to create an interest in chemistry in the students. Many students fear chemistry and the sciences. A complaint often voiced is that American students are not entering the sciences. My husband sometimes comments that a majority of the students in his department are foreign students, particularly Asian students. One question that arises during our discussion is, "Why aren't more American students pursuing the sciences?" The small numbers of American students who pursue the sciences may be due to the lack of an appreciation of the sciences along with a fear of the sciences. I must admit I feared the sciences when I was in secondary school. I found biology boring in elementary school. Chemistry was hard to grasp in high school. I am a person who needs to know why. I sought for an answer to the why of chemistry, the why of studying chemistry, but I did not receive the answer in high school. The response I often received is, "You do it because it is required." I was presented with facts and told I must learn those facts. I found the whole experience rather taxing. Looking back, I now realize that I was seeking a meaning to chemistry. I began to enjoy chemistry after I was given this perspective. I now delight in chemistry and enjoy discussing it with my husband. I am sure I am not the only student who just got through high school chemistry in order to get a passing grade.

A mystique continues to surround the sciences. We automatically assume that anyone majoring in the sciences is very intelligent. We assume that someone has to be of a higher intelligence in order to understand the sciences. The sciences are often portrayed as something beyond the reach of the ordinary individual. What is the origin of this misconception, and is this misconception being perpetuated in our schools? This misconception is often fostered by the manner in which the sciences are being taught in our elementary and secondary school. I grew up in a small community where a state college was located. I remember often being in awe of the science professors. I took a physics course in college as a requirement and loved it. In fact, I received an "A" in the course. I never considered the possibility of majoring in physics, because somewhere or sometime during my early years I developed a fear of science. I viewed it as something out of my reach. My education or miseducation regarding science had indeed begun at an early age. American children are getting the impression that the sciences are something to be avoided. From where does this impression come?

Are our students being confronted with the why of science in their classes, or are their science classes merely something to be gotten through? American students have not developed an appreciation of science and the workings of science in their everyday activities. Magic shows or activities which use concepts from the sciences should be given in the elementary schools, possibly beginning with the third grade. The desire is to arouse an interest in the students. Let's show our students how science works for them. Let's introduce our students to science at an early age. My husband once mentioned to me that he was given a chemistry set as a gift when he was in elementary school.

School, A Reflection of Society

Our social values and the very nature of our society are reflected in our schools. Our schools are mere reflections of our society. It is impossible to talk about or discuss our schools and what is "supposedly" wrong with them without discussing our society and what is wrong with it. Our schools are not perfect, but neither is our society. Changes in our society are reflected in our schools. This is better grasped if we view our schools from a utilitarian prospective. Let's consider the ways in which school aids society and the individual. In school the individual learns skills, tools, etc., for meeting his/her basic needs. School teaches an individual the things he/she needs to know. The first and foremost aim of education is to meet the needs of society. The most important goal or aim of any social order is to maintain itself. If it is to maintain itself a society needs a loyal citizenry who cherishes and upholds the nation's ideals. Our schools attempt to develop students who will become loyal and productive citizens. From the moment a child enters school he/she is taught about the nation and its ethical ideals. The elementary student learns to recite the "Pledge to the Flag." Later his/her studies teach him/her about national and state history. He/she is also taught about the operation and function of the state and national government. If the school does a thorough job, upon graduation from high school the student will be ready to participate as a responsible member of society.

An informed citizenry is necessary for the growth and maintenance of our society. As a result of more sophisticated communication devices, we are continuously made aware of other nations of the world and their effect upon us. We accept the truth that America is not the center of the earth. Our citizens must be able to interact with and communicate with other nations throughout the world. We must be aware of events in other places and how these events affect us. In other words, we must have a global perspective. Hence the emphasis upon multiculture education, and the often sounded criticism that our students are not as aware of other nations as they should be. We are often told that one responsibility of our schools is to develop an informed citizenry. Thus school is being used as a tool of socialization.

Our society must continue to maintain an educated and technologically aware citizenry if it is going to continue to compete with other nations. We are at the close of the 20th century. To subsist in our society an individual must be able to read and write. But in addition to that he/she must be able to function in a technological society. Thus we have the introduction of the computer in elementary grades. At one time in our nation's history America was the most educated and technologically sophisticated nation in the world. We were the forerunners. At the end of the 20th century things have begun to change as other nations have begun to compete with us. The panic button is sometimes pushed. Some have begun to question the productivity of our schools. Attempts are being made to increase the productivity of our students. We can no longer take our place in the world for granted. Some might feel that our schools are being pressured. Once again, our schools are serving as tools of socialization necessary to the maintenance of our social order.

Our nation needs individuals who are continually developing, testing and, when feasible, implementing new ideas as well as modifying and updating old ones. We live in a world which is rapidly changing. If we are to continue to maintain our competitive edge, we must continue to produce creative individuals. We must develop and reward creativity in our students. Thus the criticism as other nations once considered under-developed have begun to offer technological innovations, etc., that our schools are failing. Are our schools failing or is it that what was necessary in the past to maintain predominance is no longer enough in the present, and definitely will not be enough in the future? In other words it is not that our schools are failing, but other nations are beginning to catch up. Therefore we must run a little faster and work a little harder if we are to maintain our lead. Thus the need to reward creativity and to instill a love of science in our students at the elementary grades.

If our nation is going to continue to grow and maintain itself it will need citizens who are morally responsible. Respect for human life, honesty, and responsibility are essential characteristics that our nation must have in its citizenry if it is to continue to maintain itself as a civilized nation. It is sometimes asserted that the teaching of morals should not be the responsibility of the schools; rather, it should be the responsibility of the home. That may be true, but the burden of teaching morals such as respect for human life, honesty, and responsibility has gradually shifted to the schools. Thus, school is again used as a tool of socialization.

Our nation needs citizens who are altruistic and are willing to care for the sick and the aged. If a society is to be humane, it must care for the sick, the aged and those who are unable to care for themselves. At one time in our nation's history these responsibilities were fulfilled in the family and the local community. Our society has changed. We are no longer primarily a rural society. For all intents and purposes the extended family is no more. Thus we have governmental and voluntary programs which respond to the needs of the sick and the aged. Some question the need of these programs, but the programs are necessary if our society is to continue to remain humane. Thus the school's mission is to educate the population regarding the why of these programs. School is indeed a tool of socialization.

The Changing Nature of Work and the Subsequent Influence Upon Our Schools

The nature of work within our social order is changing. That affects our schools and what is taught in our school. Our changing social order and attitudes are reflected in our schools. They are reflected in our textbooks. Boyer and Savagean, (1989, p. 52) note:

> In 1948, 48 million people had jobs. In 1977, 80 million people were working. Today the number exceeds 100 million. In each year over the past three decades, there have been more people working than the year before. Workers whose trade lost out to technological change include millions of farmers, hundreds of thousands of self-employed grocers, thousands of blacksmiths, furriers, railroad conductors and locomotive engineers, sailors and deck hands. Think about it, the invention of the airplane created a whole new job market. The number of men and women who are working has increased at a faster rate than the population since the end of World War II.

The changing nature of work directly affects what is being taught in our schools. Schools are tools of socialization which prepare students with the necessary skills they will need to obtain and maintain employment. Courses taught are built around the everyday world and the needs of the market place. For instance, our work force now needs computer literate individuals, as more and more computers are being installed in the workplace. Our schools have responded by introducing computers in the elementary grades and providing computer instruction at the secondary level. It has become evident that our students need to learn certain Eastern languages as our society has begun to do more trading with Asian nations. For instance, Japan is a major trading partner. We can no longer ignore the Japanese language. The idea is being discussed that our schools should include the Japanese language in their foreign language program. Our curriculum will continue to modify itself in accordance with the employment needs of society and the market place.

Equal Educational Opportunity Reflected in Our Schools

The concept of equal educational opportunity is based on the premise that all men are created equal and therefore should have an equal access to an education. This belief has had far reaching consequences for our schools because schools can no longer separate students on the basis of race. Schools are now required to educate the handicapped in accordance with their particular handicap. The concept of equal educational opportunity does not require that all students have the same education in the same manner. Rather, it requires that all students have the right to an education in accordance with their abilities. Schools are now required to provide wheel chair ramps for students who need them. They are also required to provide special education classes for the mentally handicapped in the "least restrictive environment." These modifications alone have increased the number of students who now attend school. Today many students who are attending school would not have been able to do so 40 years ago.

Is it true that in American Society each individual has an equal educational opportunity and an equal opportunity to succeed regardless of social class, wealth or the lack of wealth? Does the student's social class or his or her race have an influence upon the education he/she receives? Student opportunities for success are greater if they have parents who are supportive, if they have been exposed to the culture around them, and if they have parents or other support groups who are able to provide enriching experiences for them. How many youth upon leaving school step into jobs that have been prepared for them and are waiting for them? These youth have a head start, and this must not be forgotten. Equal educational opportunity is provided by taking into consideration the student's particular strengths and weaknesses and then building an educational curriculum around that.

Women and the Projection of Women in Our Schools

As one time in our society, women did not work. Girls were raised to be wives and mothers. A woman's place was considered to be in the home. Going back even further, at one time women did not even vote. During the initial development of our schools, girls did not attend school to the degree that boys did. World War II was the catalyst that began to change the perception of women in our society as women began to enter the work force. This changed over a number of years and is today reflected in our schools.

The increase of women in the work force has affected our educational programs. As a result of the increased numbers of women in the work force there are no longer sex-oriented courses and activities specifically for girls and activities specifically for boys. When the authors were in high school some courses such as home economics were specifically for girls and courses such as shop and agriculture were specifically for boys. Women are now a part of the work force that must be reckoned with and considered when planning the curriculum. Women have said that they want to have access to the same jobs as men and therefore the same training as men. This has also affected the manner in which women are portrayed in textbooks.

School and the Needs of the Individual

Maslow identified the needs of the individual in his *Hierarchy of Needs.* The first and primary need of the individual is the satisfaction of his hunger. The individual needs food. Our society has changed with urbanization. The family farm has all but disappeared. People no longer have the space or the room to maintain small family gardens; therefore people are now required to purchase all or most of all of their food from others, and this takes money. When growing up we were poor and could not afford a lot of things, but the one thing I remember is we always had plenty of food to eat because my grandparents farmed. Prior to buying a freezer, my grandmother used to can food every spring and summer. When my grandmother got older, her children purchased a freezer for her. One of our goals during the spring and summer months was to fill the freezer with food for the fall and winter.

In school the student learns skills which will allow him/her to provide food for himself through employment outside the home. As our society has become more technical, specific skills are now required for most jobs. These skills require training which is acquired in our schools.

After satisfying his/her hunger need, the individual becomes concerned about his/her safety needs, i.e., need for shelter, etc. Man needs shelter to protect him/her from the harshness of the environment. As the small farm has disappeared and as more people have moved into urban areas, housing has become more expensive. The homeless and homeless families are a problem. The feeling of smugness in having a home and a job is fast disappearing as people confront the fact that they would be homeless in a few months if they were to lose their jobs. Homelessness was not a problem twenty years ago. Rising inflation has contributed to the problem of the homeless.

The aim of education is to prepare the individual to meet hunger and safety needs by equipping him/her with the skill and training that will allow him/her to obtain employment, or to satisfy his/her hunger and safety needs in a socially-approved manner. We prefer that our youth obtain employment rather than steal from others. I often experience a sense of well-being when I encounter garbage collectors because these are often young men who have chosen to work regardless of how menial the task, rather than sell drugs or steal. I often wonder what would happen if individuals refused to work, but rather chose to steal to meet their needs and desires. What would happen to our society? The individual, who is willing to work for a living, no matter how menial the job, is to be congratulated.

Transition From School to the World of Work

Many of our students are very naive about life. They are growing up with a false perception of reality or a Hollywood mentality. Some are growing up without an appreciation of work or responsibility. Some know very little about life or what it takes to succeed in life.

I was talking with a young man who had recently married. His wife was pregnant. He told me about how difficult it was to "make ends meet on his salary." During our conversation, he made an interesting statement. He said he "wished his mother had made him study more rather than allow him to play freely in the neighborhood." I am sure that at the time he was playing freely in the neighborhood, his friends who were required to study, to do their homework and to keep their grades up, envied him. He gave no thought to the future or his future well being. He was having a good time.

After observing life around me I sometimes think it would have been best if some individuals had remained children. I say this because some individuals although mature physically are not mature emotionally. They are unable to assume responsibility for themselves or others. Some are unable to keep a job after obtaining one. It would be good if these individuals could remain children in the care of their parents, but we must grow up and assume the responsibilities of adults. A greater part of our life is spent as adults than is spent as children. Because of this, it is the responsibility of our parents and our teachers to prepare us to assume adult roles. It is wrong to allow a child to grow up naive about the world around him and what it takes to succeed. School serves that purpose. Some individuals live in a storybook world. Parents often attempt to shelter their children from the harsh realities of life. For example, often when parents are laid off from their job, they will do everything that can be done to shield this information from their children. Their desire is to act as if nothing has happened. Their reasoning is that children are too young to be confronted with the unpleasant aspects of life. It might be better to explain the situation to the children. Children need to experience life as it really is and not live a fairy tale life from which they are suddenly forced to awaken after leaving school or after graduating from high school.

Some parents hate to tell their children that they, the parents, cannot afford to buy them a particular item. There is nothing wrong with parents telling their child that they cannot afford a particular toy. Children need to develop an idea of the value of money and an understanding of our capitalist system. The purpose of giving a child an allowance is to aid the child in the development of an understanding of the usage and management of money.

Some students, for the first time in their lives, are asked to think about what they intend to do after completing high school or leaving school before the completion of their studies. Of course the higher achievers have already made their future plans. The message is often communicated by parents to students that their free stay is over. "Mom and dad will not continue to carry you; Mom and Dad will continue a little longer if you choose to go to college or junior college," is the message they often receive. The failure here is not in our schools but in our culture. Our schools merely reflect our culture. Students have been taught for twelve years, but the question is what have they been taught about the real world and how to survive in it.

I can remember leaving home and going off to college. Initially I was very excited. Soon I experienced a traumatic shudder, when I realized I was miles away from home and away from support groups. I had to confront things that I had never confronted before, i.e., the cost of housing and food. These were topics which were not discussed in my high school civics classes. I knew that someone paid the bills, but I never stopped to wonder who or why.

School and the acquisition of a high school education is not an end; it is merely a means to an end. Some would say that the student's completion of high school ends the school's responsibility to the student, but I say no. Students need assistance in making the transition from school to the world of work. Counselors and others work diligently with students who plan to continue on to college. Enter a high school guidance office and you will find college catalogs. What about the student who does not plan to continue on to college? That student needs help in making the transition from school to the world of work. Students need to be taught how to look for a job and how to complete a job application. Students need to be aided in making the transition from school to work. This could become a part of the vocational education program.

Chapter Five

THE RELEVANCE OF SCHOOL

At one time in our national history schools were primarily for the wealthy. It was automatically assumed that children of the wealthy would be sent to school while children of the poor received little if any formal education. There was no free public education or mandatory attendance laws. Eventually the public education system developed, and compulsory attendance laws were formulated to guarantee that all children would attend school. Public schools were lengthened to include the secondary school. It was later determined that some type of certification was needed to document that the individual had completed secondary school requirements, thus the high school diploma. At one time in our national history the individual could easily obtain employment without having completed or having received a high school diploma. Little if any negative status was attached to not having earned the high school diploma, but gradually this has changed.

Until recently, individuals could obtain employment without a high school diploma. It has now become difficult if not impossible to obtain employment without a high school diploma. One of the first things an applicant is often asked on a job application is to provide information about the high school he or she attended and the date the high school diploma was received. Applicants are asked to provide information about their high school education, regardless of how menial the job for which they are applying. To not complete high school is perceived by many as a failure to complete the process of certification that the individual is ready to participate in and compete in the larger society. What about the youngster who says, "Look I don't want to waste my time in high school. I have tried it and it is boring." Does he or she have the freedom to say this without negative consequences? The answer is "no." During the early years of our educational system he or she had the opportunity to say this without negative consequences, but that is not the case today.

Society develops standards for its members. Those who expect to successfully compete in society must be willing to master those standards. There was a time in our history when we were often presented with success stories of men and women who had made it "to the top" without having completed high school or who had little if any formal schooling. That is no longer acceptable because society's expectations have changed.

This chapter was begun with the intent of demonstrating the relevance of school by highlighting the relationship between the completion of school and subsequent employment. Further investigation of this relationship, led the writer to question the absoluteness and the degree of the relationship. Is the completion of high school a guarantee of subsequent employment? Students, particularly those at risk of dropping out of school, want to know the benefits of staying in school. Can we guarantee students' future employment upon their successfully completing school? Should future job earnings be the incentive and the only reason for staying in and completing school? The answer to both questions is "no."

Youth are given a brief rest period upon completion of high school before they are asked to assume additional responsibilities. Their parents expect them to eventually contribute to their support if they do not plan to continue their education. Surprisingly, the majority of youth are not asked to contribute to their support, unless they are poor and the added income is needed, until they have either completed high school or dropped out of high school. This is an unwritten rule. They are often not asked to contribute to their support if they decide to continue on to college. The student is called upon to make a major decision upon completing high school. That decision and the choices made will affect them throughout their life. That decision is "whether to get a job now or to pursue further schooling". The student is often asked to choose among alternatives which should have been investigated in high school but were not. Some choose to delay that choice and to obtain additional information. What about the student who drops out of school? He or she has already made a decision. Students who drop out of school are expected to obtain full-time employment. The question is "have they learned anything in school that will prepare them for this major undertaking?" Often, the answer is "no." Why haven't they learned anything in school to prepare them for entrance into the adult world? Is it because our schools are designed primarily to prepare students for further schooling beyond high school?

For many students, the completion of high school will end their formal education. High school should have prepared these individuals to make the transition into mainstream society as functioning members. The question is often asked, "What skills and knowledge does the individual need to possess in order to become a functioning member of society?" He or she should have a knowledge of the workings of society. Political science courses in junior and senior high school attempt to provide introductory information about our political and social system. The individual should possess the minimum basic skills needed to function within society. Those skills should be congruent with the social order and the demands of the social order. He or she should have been provided a history of our society. The history of the society provides a framework in which to compare events which may occur within society or within his or her life.

We are often told our youth are failing and dropping out of school before earning their high school diploma. There has been an increase in school violence, drug usage and crime with few solutions to these problems being provided. Today we are often told our schools are failing our youth. We are also reminded that our youth and our schools don't compare to Japanese youth and schools. Maybe before making negative comparisons we should clarify the ways in which our schools are different from Japanese schools. One important way is that in our schools everyone has an opportunity for an equal education. There is no forced track based upon student achievement. It is important that the individual remember that the operation of the school system and the goals of the school system will affect the outcome of the school system. We are also reminded that our schools are falling short in preparing our youth for subsequent employment.

Schreiber (1965, p. 23) made an interesting observation. He noted that "the varied campaigns to get youths to stay in school can only be successful if they are unsuccessful; for if everyone went on to graduate from high-school and if many went on to college, there would not be enough appropriate jobs available." It is dangerous to raise aspirations if we cannot guarantee a payoff for the additional effort involved. Completing high school should mean more than preparing to get a job. Hopefully the acquisition of a job is not the only carrot we are presenting students as a reason for staying in school. What happens to the individual who is unable to obtain a job upon completion of high school? Has his high school education and the effort involved in its acquisition been a failure? The answer is "no," and that is why we need to define and present students with other reasons for completing high school besides obtaining a job.

The Value of a High School Degree

A question which remains to be answered is what does the individual gain from attending school if he or she does not plan to attend college? Are our schools merely baby-sitting students until they are ready to leave home and take care of themselves? Are we attempting to develop individuals who will be able to function within society and more importantly, contribute to the present society? These questions may be summarized in the one question, "How is school as it is presently organized relevant to the student and the society?" Some, particularly youth, may believe that the educational system is a "monster" which must be wrestled with and overcome whether they like the system or not. So many advantages of our culture hinge on whether or not the individual has successfully completed the educational program. Rather than asking, "Is our educational system relevant to the needs of today's youth; maybe we should ask, "What are the rewards of successfully completing the educational system?" One such reward is often the opportunity to apply for and obtain work. In many instances the job applicant who has not successfully obtained his/her high school education is not even considered as a job candidate.

Another reward which is often overlooked is that the student has been indoctrinated and prepared to function within the larger society. Hopefully a high school education presents the individual with the minimum knowledge and skills he or she will need to function within our society. Alexander, Natriello and Pallas (1985) completed research which addressed whether the cognitive performance of youth is improved as a result of their being in school. Their results indicate that cognitive skills of youngsters who stay in school improve more than those of dropouts, and this advantage is observed across a rather broad range of skill areas. The research report emphasizes that schools do make a difference. Webster defined relevant as "having significant and demonstrable bearing on the matter at hand."

Often education, particularly post secondary education, is the stamp of approval that allows the individual to apply for and obtain certain jobs. The individual who does not possess it knows that he or she need not apply. Collins (1979, p. 3) postulated:

Education is the most important determinant yet discovered of how far one will go in today's world. Moreover, it has been growing steadily more important in the sense that each new generation of Americans has spent more and more time in school and taken jobs with higher and higher educational requirements.

Some may ask, "Does school continue to remain relevant in the life of an individual?" The answer is "yes." Regardless of how negatively people may view school, it is still relevant. Schreiber (1965) describes our world as a place "where the high school diploma assumes the function of both a certificate of employability and *carte d'entree* to those occupations less susceptible to unemployment." Is it necessary for an individual to have completed at least 12 years of formal education? It may not be necessary in some countries, but it is necessary in America.

The question is often asked, "Are schools preparing youth to function in our technological society?" The answer is "yes." Unskilled jobs are disappearing in our society. With increased technology, jobs require increased skills. Youngsters who leave school without acquiring the needed skills will have difficulty attaining employment. Another factor is that unskilled jobs pay very little. It is difficult in our world today for individuals to support their family upon the pay of an unskilled worker. Maybe that was not the case 20 years ago, but it is the case today. This makes the obtaining of a high school education even more important.

A high school education or diploma is not a guarantee that an individual will obtain a job, rather it is only the first step toward obtaining a job that will allow the individual to support himself/herself and his/her family. This needs to be stated. It is merely certification that the individual has passed the minimum requirements established by school systems in the nation. Tyler (1965, p. 5) summarized our concerns with the dropout. He noted that the concern with the dropout largely arises from the following factors:

1. Employment opportunities are greatly limited for the youth who is not a high school graduate. Hence, he/she represents a large proportion of the unemployed youth and young adults.

2. It is difficult for the contemporary school dropout to achieve a sense of individual worth and belonging to the larger community, particularly in the large city.

3. There is an apparent tendency toward rigidity in residential and educational segregation which shakes our confidence in the prospect of

future improvement, e.g., confidence in the prospect of future improvement, such as occurred among previous immigrant groups.

4. A general view that the public school's role is to educate all—at least through high school—has developed. Hence, dropout implies failure on the school's part, particularly when a large percentage of dropouts clearly has the mental ability to succeed.

Entry into Higher Education

The student who desires to pursue a professional career must possess a high school diploma before entry into higher education. Students who have demonstrated higher achievement are often allowed to take certain college courses for credit while they are attending high school. There is nothing wrong with this practice if the student has demonstrated that he or she is able to master the course material. What about the individual who leaves school before obtaining a high school diploma? That individual must return to high school or obtain a GED before even beginning to pursue college work. The high school diploma has become a "rite of passage."

Relevance of School for the Social Order

Something which is not often mentioned or discussed is that students staying in school also benefit society. There are economic, social and political reasons the larger society would like to have youth remain in school. What are youth going to do with their free time if they don't spend it in school? This was not a problem or a concern when children worked as a matter of course. That is no longer the case. School and the acquisition of vital skills is important for the development of the individual. Rogers (1989) noted that the educational system should help the individual to meet minimum standards in other basic subjects that are necessary for survival and effective functioning in society. Pellicano (1987) encourages a reexamination of the original value structure of schools to ascertain whether that structure is still valid for today's schools.

Relevance of the Curriculum

The curriculum must be continually modified and the methodologies updated in accord with our changing society and its needs. As the computer has become the mainstream of our society, schools have begun to install computers in the classrooms. They are in both elementary and high schools. All students regardless of whether they plan to pursue a higher degree should be required to take an introductory computer course. A majority of schools has made this a requirement. A more advanced computer course should be available to those students who plan to pursue a college degree or those who want more detailed training. This practice should be implemented in all of our schools, especially our inner city schools. Anyone who hopes to obtain a job in our present society and our future society will be required to possess a computer competency.

Young men and women, especially those who do not plan to pursue advanced training should be taught skills which will allow them to obtain clerical employment. When the authors were in high school during the 1960s, employers at a minimum wanted prospective clerical and secretarial employees to possess typing skills. This is no longer enough. A review of the help wanted ads reveals that employers seeking clerical staff now expect them not only to be familiar with the word processor but also to possess a competency on it. This change in employer requirements has facilitated a need for modification of business or clerical courses in our high schools. A rising number of employers are replacing the electric typewriter with computers. Students should be introduced to the word processor in high school. Some might argue that the high school is not and should not be a vocational school and the authors would agree to a certain degree. Those arguing that the high school is not a vocational school might argue that those wanting job skills should attend a vocational school upon completion of high school. What about the individual who must begin full time employment upon completion of high school?

We should change promotional advertisements, often used to keep students from dropping out of high school, if students are not going to acquire elementary job skills while in high school. Students from poor and disadvantaged homes and middle-class homes are concerned about future job earnings. It is not enough for them to learn Shakespeare. They want something they can use to make money. Schools say that they are preparing youngsters to enter into the mainstream society as contributing adults. These youngsters must learn to take care of themselves before they will be able to contribute anything to society.

Students need to be made aware of the knowledge and skills needed to successfully compete in the adult world. This knowledge and these skills cannot be fully obtained in 12 years as our schools are presently organized. We must move from the abstract to the concrete. Our students must acquire an awareness of the functioning of our society. This awareness must not be something that affects somebody else but does not affect the student. Many of them watch the news. The authors watched the news when they were in high school. Although pictures flashed regarding the Vietnam War, the war meant very little. Vietnam was somewhere "over there," and the United States was "over here." Much of the news continues to be irrelevant to adolescents. High school students continue to take social studies and civics courses just as the authors took social studies and civics courses when they were in high school. These courses often presented information regarding how our social and political systems are supposed to work, rather than how they actually work.

The teacher, one of the author's remembers most from her high school days, was a civics teacher, who was loved by all of his students. The students loved him because his classes were interesting and stimulating. He made the students think. He used examples from our everyday experiences. For example, when discussing the consequences of crime, he presented an example of an individual, more than likely a youth, who used a gun to rob a gas station. The individual, when apprehended, was tried for armed robbery, which is a serious crime. Another individual used a gun to rob a bank. When apprehended, this individual was also tried for armed robbery. The individual who robbed a gas station acquired a few hundred dollars, if that much money. The individual who robbed a bank, more than likely acquired a few thousand dollars. When apprehended, both were charged with armed robbery. That example, along with others, provided the students information about the different types of crime along with the consequences. He attempted to teach his students about our criminal justice system by giving up examples to which we could relate. We need more courses which focus upon an examination of current issues.

One of the authors remembers taking a family life course in college. Let's offer more family life courses in high school. High school students need business and economic courses. They need courses which explain to them how our capitalist system works. The majority of high school students have never thought about their personal upkeep because of the assumption that somebody (their parents) will provide everything they need. The authors are often saddened when they hear about youth who run away from home, because the authors realize that the youth are not aware of the significance of what they have done. The youth have undertaken a major step. They have left the security of home. Their needs have not changed, but the providers of their needs will change. Youth, particularly those who run away from home before completing school, are often shocked to discover what is involved in living on their own and being independent. They are now responsible for their personal upkeep, the rent and food. Often they have never thought about these things before striking out upon their own. Maybe our youth should be presented with more information about what is needed to survive in our society as part of their regular studies. Let's teach our math courses by using practical everyday examples to which youth can relate. The National Council of Teachers of Mathematics (NCTN) standards released in March 1989, emphasized that math instruction should focus on skill application rather than rote drill and computation. The NCTM emphasized that this is a response to mathematical demands of the workplace.

Benedict, Snell and Miller (1987) described Enterprise High, a unique curriculum begun in Michigan, which simulated life outside school, to show students how education affects their ability to earn a living and manage their lives. That is good, because students need to be made aware of the ways in which the acquisition of an education affects their ability to earn a living and function in society. Many students leave school without giving much thought to how they are going to earn a living and solve life's problems. Youth should be forced to think about these things. These issues are often not raised until the youth reaches his senior year. These issues are often sooner raised for the high achieving student by his/her parents and his/her guidance counselors as they emphasize that he/she should begin to think about applying to college. What about the average student who is not especially interested in attending college? Should these issues have been raised before he/she reached his or her senior year? Maybe if these issues had been raised earlier he or she may have begun to give serious thought to attending college or a professional school.

Students should be introduced to career days in junior high school and even elementary school. They need to be made aware of the various career options and what is required for these careers. We must encourage our youth to think about the why of school and how they intend to manage their future lives. This emphasis, beginning in junior high, will affect the number of youth who drop out as they learn that there is nothing waiting out there for the youth who drops out of school before acquiring his high school diploma, and often the high school diploma is just the first step.

Our country is in a period of economic slowdown, some might even call it a recession. How many high school students are aware of what a recession is? How many high school students are aware of how a recession affects our economy? Students need to be aware of these issues. Maybe that was not the case when work was plentiful. Work is no longer plentiful. Let's be "real" with the youth of today. Remember, we don't want our youth entering the larger adult world with the "feeling" that they have been deceived.

Education for Employment

Education has become even more relevant today as available jobs have become more dependent upon the individual possessing certain skills and abilities. Projections for the year 2000 indicate that new jobs will require a work force whose median level of education is 13.5 years. On the average, workers who fill these jobs will have to have some college training. Jobs in which a large proportion of workers have less than four years of high school are among the slowest growing and poorest paying in the economy, being out paced by jobs requiring higher levels of mathematics, language, and reading skills (America's Shame, America's Hope, Twelve Million Youth at Risk).

A number of jobs in the least-skilled categories will disappear, while many high-skilled professions will grow. Overall the skill mix of the economy will be rapidly moving upscale and increasing numbers of workers will be required to have computer, basic academic, problem solving, and interpersonal skills. (Collins (1979, p. 3) determined:

> Of all those variables that are easily measurable, education (usually indicated simply by the number of years in school) has been found to be the most important predictor of occupational success, along with parents' occupation itself, and much of the effect of parents' occupation level appears to operate through its effect on children's education.... In 1937–1938, 11% of employers required high school diplomas or more for skilled laborers; in the 1945–46 period, this had risen to 19%; and in 1967 to 32%. For clerical jobs, the percentage requiring high school or more rose more slowly: 57% in 1937–38; 56–72% in 1945–46; 72% in 1967.

Our concern focuses upon youth who leave school without the foundation necessary to obtain adequately paying and secure jobs.

School and the Real World

The question is often asked, is school relevant for this generation? Is it meeting the needs of today's youth? Benedict, Snell and Miller (1987, p. 76) reported that "dropouts complained that school seemed irrelevant to them, they could find no connection between the things they were being asked to learn in school and the so-called real world."

It is evident that the youth of today are seeking answers. When asked to do something, they often ask why and what is its purpose. Do we have answers to give youth when they question the purpose of school? When I was in school I saw no real meaning or purpose of it. I merely went because it was required and expected of me. I studied hard and got good grades because I knew my parents wanted me to, and I knew it was expected of me. In other words I did not question my parents nor the dictates of school. I assumed that because I was a child and they were adults they knew what was best for me. Anyone who has a youngster knows that the youth of today do not hesitate to question them. They want to know why. Are we prepared to give them answers regarding the relevance of school for them? Today's youth will not merely go along with the expectations of authority figures. Today's youth must be presented with the connection between what they are doing in the classroom and how it will affect them in the real world.

Justiz and Kameen (1987) related the success story of Kevin, who by the 10th grade had compiled a record of four arrests, and seemed likely to drop out. Kevin enrolled in a special program, Peninsula Academies, a business/school partnership for potential dropouts in California's Santa Clara Valley. They noted that for the first time in Kevin's life, through the Academies' integration of work experience with academic study, school became relevant for Kevin. It was not enough for Kevin to merely attend school. School had to be made relevant to Kevin.

I began my professional career as an assistant professor of psychology. When explaining conditioning to my students as well as many other behavioral theories, I chose examples that were relevant to them. When explaining the effect of reinforcement on subsequent behavior, I often used the example of a man who observed flowers (stimuli) in a window while strolling down the street. He stopped to buy some flowers for his wife (response). When he arrived home, he presented the flowers to her. Her reaction (reinforcement) determined whether she continued to receive flowers. More than likely she continued to receive flowers if she reacted lovingly and cheerfully to the flowers. If she reacted negatively she probably received no more flowers. The students loved the example because it was something to which they could relate.

The Purpose of School

Students want to know about the purpose of school, and they are not too young to learn about the history of formal education as well as the purpose of school. Maybe we don't tell them because we have not stopped to think about or examine the purpose of school. What are our schools as they are presently organized seeking to accomplish? Are our schools merely baby-sitting youth until they are 18 and able to go out into the world and take care of themselves? Are schools attempting to develop individuals who will be able to contribute to the social order and to function within the present society and even more importantly, contribute to that society? In other words, what are schools trying to do? Why do we require youngsters to complete 12 years of school before they are allowed to receive a high school diploma? These are questions that should be addressed by parents and educators. We should be able to respond to youth when they ask us why they must go to school. It is not enough to merely say, "Because it is required." We must give them rational reasons.

Educational Reform

A report from the Business Advisory Committee of the States (BACES, 1985, p. 5) indicated:

> Leaders in education are called upon to "get it right the first time," head off disconnection with effective early education, alternative schools and dropout prevention programs. Schools are challenged to move education reform into a new phase that connects at-risk students more directly with adults and the larger worlds of work and culture.

An education reform movement in the 1980s which began with the publication of the National Commission on Excellence in Education's report, *A Nation at Risk,* reads this way: "The educational foundations of our society are presently being eroded by a rising tide of mediocrity that threatens our very future as a nation and a people."

The emphasis in our society is upon succeeding. I sometimes wonder if the motto is not "succeed at any cost." Succeed whether you like yourself or not, just succeed. Our schools are reflections of society and often reflect this motto. This motto has carried over into our schools, with the increased emphasis upon test scores and grades. What about studying to understand what you are taking? What about putting under-standing before merely earning a grade? We admire the individual who stands up to the "so-called system" and says this is not for me, I want to understand. I recently took a computer course. It was a course that I took for professional improvement. I didn't need the grade; in fact I took the course because I wanted to understand computers more. When test time came around, I reacted like a student whose degree depended upon the course. I studied, but was my studying for understanding or was it merely memorizing facts by studying what I thought was going to be on the test? With the near paranoic emphasis upon grades in our schools, maybe we should place more emphasis upon understanding concepts and less emphasis upon grades. This would encourage the C student to aim for understanding as opposed to beating himself/herself over the head because they are not "A" students.

Chapter Six

THE DROPOUT—WHAT ARE THE REFORMS?

Is there a difference between the education offered to youth during the development of our educational systems and the education provided youth today?" The answer is, "yes." Such differences are:

1. Compulsory school attendance,
2. Varied ethnic and racial groups within the culture,
3. More information to learn,
4. More students in school,
5. Students entering school at an earlier age,
6. Efforts to provide equal educational opportunity for all individuals regardless of race or handicap

Today school dropouts are often viewed negatively. The unspoken assumption is that they have failed or our schools have failed them. However, students leaving school before completing their educational program and earning a diploma (dropouts) is nothing new in our country. They have always existed. What has changed is the response of our society to students who leave school before completing their educational program. The value of an education has increased. As the value of an education increases, it's almost impossible for anyone to survive and function in our society without possessing certain basic skills and knowledge.

It is no longer enough for a person to read at the third grade level or to merely recognize words. To survive and compete in today's society a person must be able to read fluently and understand what he or she reads. Also, the individual needs to possess basic math skills, in addition to having both a knowledge and understanding of the world around him or her. The criticism is often made that youngsters are not able to recognize and locate many of the countries which are discussed on the daily news. Even when presented a globe, they are unable to locate these countries. This kind of failure is unacceptable, especially since the knowledge base needed to function effectively within our society has changed and continues to change.

School is one of the mechanisms used to educate students. One of its goals is to prepare students to move into society as responsible individuals. The desire is to equip students with competences which will enable them to function within the larger society in which they live. Those skills and the nature of those skills changed as society moved from a primarily agricultural society to an industrial society, then to a technological society. Jobs disappeared and others came into existence. So, literacy became a necessity for individuals if they were to function effectively within the social order.

As our society advanced during the technological age, the competencies and skills needed to function within the workplace also changed. At one time in our history, it was possible for individuals to work and earn a living without possessing the ability to read or write. As for a personal experience, I remember as a little girl my grandparents were unable to sign their names. They were able only to scribble their names. That was acceptable because it was understood that they had received little formal schooling. That was nothing of which to be ashamed. They were able to function and to support their family. I wrote for them when I grew older. Of course their lack of formal education would not be acceptable today.

The technological age has eliminated a number of menial jobs. The advent of the computer has made it necessary for individuals in many jobs to possess the ability to master the computer or at least develop a computer proficiency on their jobs. Our high schools have reacted by providing computer classes. Also, computers have been installed in our elementary schools.

In order to function within our society, today, one needs to be computer literate. Most clerical jobs now demand that the individual know how to use a computer or word processor. When the computer was first mass marketed, companies were willing to train their employees on the computer. This is no longer the case with many companies. The assumption is that basic computer skills have been taught in high school. So employees receive on-the-job training in using the company's new software packages.

PUBLIC EDUCATION: YESTERDAY AND TODAY

Our public education system in America is approximately 150 years old. The first common or public schools were developed in the Northern states before the Civil War. The common school movement of the 19th

Century was one of the major events in American industrial, social, and educational history. Although defined in various ways, common schools were publicly supported and controlled institutions that offered a curriculum of reading, writing, arithmetic, grammar, history, geography, and health. Schools served and continue to serve a necessary purpose. They instilled the values of punctuality, hard work, and industry. Gutek, (1988) identified the functional role of the early schools in the United States as preparing individuals for life in a technological society of growing complexity and specialization. According to him schools prepared people to contribute to an emerging technological society by stressing work, diligence, punctuality, and perseverance.

Compulsory School Attendance

Compulsory attendance laws were passed to guarantee that all individuals would have access to an education. Parents could no longer keep their children at home. With the advent of compulsory attendance laws, parents were now responsible for their children's attendance at school. "Massachusetts led the nation in 1852 in passing a state-wide compulsory attendance law; therefore, by 1900, 32 states had followed suit, and by 1920 all states in the United States had compulsory attendance laws" (Beck, 1964, p. 90).

Schreiber, (1965, p. 30) emphasizes that "most of the students who now drop out would have never been in school fifty years ago." Compulsory attendance laws and the implementation of those laws guarantee that all children would be provided a "free public education." All children regardless of race or economic status are required to attend school. Because of the current emphasis upon the dropout, along with the increase in the number of dropout prevention programs, some may think that the numbers of dropouts are increasing. If we examine the number of dropouts over the years, we will soon discover that the relative number of dropouts is decreasing. Writing in 1965, Schreiber (p. 20) noted that "we may talk about the dropout, but this century has witnessed a steady and impressive growth in school retention rates, i.e., in the proportion of 9th grade pupils who achieve their high school diplomas four years later. At the turn of the century, for instance, not more than 6 or 7 of every 100 ninth grade students graduated four years later. By 1930 the proportion had risen to one-half; at present, it stands at about two-thirds.

The problem of what to do with the dropout is new, not the fact of the occurrence of the dropout. Nationally, there has been a steady increase in the number of high school graduates. In 1870, 2.0% of 17 year olds graduated from high school and 1.7% attended college. In 1900, 6.4% of 17 year olds graduated from high school and 4.0% attended college. In 1920, 16.8% of 17 year olds graduated from high school and 8.9% attended college. In 1940, 50.8% of 17 year olds graduated from high school and 8.9% attended college. By 1970, 76.5% of 17 year olds graduated from high school and 52.8% attended college. A question I am left with is. "What is the dropout problem? Is it that there are no jobs for these individuals? Is it incomplete socialization? What happens to the socialization of the youth who leaves school early or leaves school before earning a diploma? Why is there an increased concern regarding dropouts when we have always had dropouts? Schreiber postulates in a 1965 publication that "the essential problem has not so much to do with numbers as with the fact that the world to which contemporary dropouts seek entrance has a diminishing place for them".

High school graduates are now filling many of the jobs that were once filled by individuals who did not complete high school. There is no longer any room for the individual who fails to complete high school. We now have an unemployment problem. Certainly, unemployment affects and to a certain degree defines the dropout problem. The percentage of individuals completing high school has steadily increased over the years, but we will continue to have a dropout problem as long as we have unemployment because during periods of high unemployment people often take jobs for which they are more than qualified, thus everyone is forced to take jobs for which they are over qualified. This pushes the individual who did not complete high school out of the job market.

Child Labor

At one time, in the history of this nation, it was assumed and even expected that children of poor working class families would not attend school, (waste their time), but rather that they would obtain employment as soon as possible to aid in family support. Beck (1965, p. 90) notes that "as late as 1920 the United States census reported a million children 10 to 15 years of age were gainfully employed." That is no longer the case. Youth cannot obtain part time employment until they are 14 years old. During the early part of this century working as opposed to going to school was not frowned upon; consequently, individuals did not go beyond elementary school. Not attending school did not make them idle because they could find gainful employment. Besides, parents who chose to withdraw their children from school were not frowned upon. Let's be honest, that is no longer the case.

What is a child or youth of today going to do if he or she does not attend school? Laws restrict the age in which a child can obtain employment. For a youngster over 14 years of age the question becomes what type of employment is he or she likely to obtain? How much money is he or she likely to earn? These problems are reflected in our educational system and the value that is attached to an education. The completion of a program of secondary education which is certified by the receipt of a high school diploma has increased in value. Schreiber (1965) noted that our world is increasingly a world "where the high school diploma assumes the function of both a certificate of employability and *carte d'entree* to those occupations less susceptible to unemployment." He further noted that the unemployment problem is indeed a prime sponsor of the dropout problem.

Education for All

The perceived role of the school and the responsibility of public education has changed. During the early history of our public school system schools were primarily for the upper and middle classes. According to Gutek (1988, p. 9) "the colonists believed in a two track system of schools—one for the poor and another for the wealthy." America is a nation of immigrants beginning with the early colonists. Our schools did not acknowledge or recognize the uniqueness of the various races. The "melting pot" theory postulated that through assimilation the various ethnic groups and races would lose their uniqueness and become one "American people." This was and is not the case.

The melting pot theory was questioned during the 1960s. Our educational system was forced to acknowledge that certain ethnic groups had not been acknowledged in our history or our social studies curriculum. It became evident that change was needed in our schools. Gutek (1988, p. 71) notes that "the respect for ethnic and social diversity, known as multuralism, reverses the patterns of earlier years when public schooling was conceived as an agency for cultural assimilation or homogenization."

The concept of education for all and the implementation of the concept of equal educational opportunity for all has greatly affected the number and type of students who are enrolled in our schools. We now educate a variable and heterogeneous group of students. We educate students of all races as well as students with varied mental capabilities from the gifted to the mentally retarded. We also educate students with learning disabilities. We attempt to develop educational programs that are congruent with the student's needs and his or her abilities.

African Americans

The early public schools in America were legally segregated. The 1954 Supreme Court decision in Brown vs. the Board of Education of Topeka, Kansas ruled that racial segregation in public schools was unconstitutional. Prior to the 1954 decision blacks and whites were educated separately and unequally. The 1954 decision was a catalyst which began the Civil Rights movement. Other special needs groups who had been ignored by the school system began to seek and to pursue their rights to an education. Now schools are required to educate these students in the least restrictive environment. Textbooks were rewritten to include the accomplishments of blacks and other minorities. Slowly our curriculum is becoming more pluralistic. The 1954 decision and the subsequent movement of blacks for "equal rights" served as a catalyst for other minorities, women and the handicapped.

Hispanic Americans

Our educational system is experiencing a steady and consistent increase in bilingual and bicultural programs. This increase in bicultural and bilingual programs in our schools is a reflection of the larger society. Hispanic and Mexican Americans are a growing minority in America. They often speak Spanish, and many of their children enter school unable to speak English. These children must be taught in both English and Spanish which is the intent of bilingual education programs.

As we acknowledge the pluralistic nature of American culture we are forced to acknowledge the need for American students to be taught about other cultures and other people. In fact, there is a growing opinion among some educators, including the writer, that American students are deficient in comparison to many foreign students because they are not taught another language besides English. Foreign languages, unfortunately, are taught most often at the secondary education level. This writer believes that foreign languages are more easily grasped if they are taught during the formative years when a student is learning his or her native language.

The American Woman

While making it illegal to discriminate against minorities, the 1964 Civil Rights Act also made it illegal to discriminate against women. The women's liberation movement which subsequently followed the 1964 Civil Rights Act demanded equal rights for women and equal treatment of men and women. These demands and subsequent reactions to these demands affected and are still affecting our educational system. Until recently our educational systems targeted certain courses and activities toward females, while other courses and activities were targeted toward males. It was assumed that some jobs were for women and some jobs were for men. With the advent of the women's liberation movement, women began to work in occupations which had previously been all male. With the advancement of equal education they began to compete with men for jobs. They demanded equal education. As more women entered the work force the number of available jobs for men began to decrease. The women's liberation movement weakened the traditional concept that there was an "appropriate" gender-based education for men and for women (Gutek, 1988, p. 84)

Children with Special Needs

Public schools were established to educate all American children. This was not an actual reality until recently. Prior to the 1964 Civil Rights Act handicapped children were neglected by our educational system. In 1971 a U.S. district court ordered Pennsylvania school districts to educate all retarded learners between the ages of 4 and 21. Mills v. Board of Education of the District of Columbia in 1972 extended the right to an education to all handicapped children and guaranteed them the right to due process protection. PL 94-142 the Education of All Handicapped Children Act of 1975, mandated that a free public education be provided to all handicapped children and that they be educated in "the least restrictive environment." We now have mainstreaming which is the integration of handicapped learners into the regular classroom.

The inclusion of children with special needs in our educational programs has increased the number of students taught in our schools.

Education of the Disadvantaged

The advent of the 1960s saw attention focused upon the disadvantaged. It was acknowledged that social class and race affected the early experiences of youngsters and their subsequent educational attainment. It was also acknowledged that some students enter school at a greater advantage than others. The 1965 Elementary and Secondary Education Act sought to address the educational needs of youngsters who are often labeled disadvantaged.

The acknowledgment of the disadvantaged, or rather the acknowledgment that all students do not enter school with the same experiences, has led to modifications in our educational programs and the inclusion of new programs. We now have Head Start programs for preschoolers and Chapter I programs for school age children.

ELEMENTARY AND SECONDARY EDUCATION

Every society regardless of how primitive it is, has a means of transmitting its knowledge, beliefs, methods and values to the younger members of the society. That method of transmission is a description of our elementary and secondary education programs. The foundations of science, social science, art, music, and physical education, are also established in the elementary school years. In preliterate societies, elementary education of a utilitarian sort was done in families or kinship groups and was enough to prepare the individual to assume a responsible position within the social order. Children learned needed skills such as fishing, farming, and cooking, etc. Literate societies such as those of ancient Greece and Rome stressed the process of becoming literate by learning to read and write the language and becoming familiar with its literature. The common schools of the 19th century stressed the fundamental skills of reading, writing, spelling, mathematics.

The essential goal of elementary education was and continues to be the preparation in fundamental skills and knowledge. Children are educated in the basic skills and the primary areas of knowledge. At one time in our nation's history, elementary education was all the education that youth received. Few students went beyond the eighth grade. The sons and daughters of immigrants often dropped out of school, as soon as it was legally possible. They frequently went to work in factories, mines, and small family-owned shops to earn money to supplement the family's income. Even African American children went to work rather than to high school. The rural poor were also usually not among those attending high school. Goodman (1964, p. 41) noted that "the 94 percent who in 1900 did not finish high school had other life opportunities, including often the possibility of making a lot of money and/or of rising in politics—though not in high policy, an area which belonged to the schooled."

Although many factors contributed to the phenomenal increase in high school attendance, the most compelling ones were social and economic. Modernization and its attendant need for persons to possess more sophisticated knowledge and technical competences made a high school education a minimal necessity for most jobs. Furthermore, the state laws that set a minimum age for beginning employment and to require compulsory school attendance have worked to keep most of the appropriate age group enrolled in school.

Vocational Education

Beck (1965, p. 91) notes, "It took the need for skilled labor, made manifest by World War I, to win from Congress federal support of vocational education; the Smith-Hughes Act became law in February, 1917, inaugurating a succession of enactments that reimbursed states for the teaching of vocational agriculture, home economics, and industrial arts." Vocational education is now a viable part of the secondary school curriculum. Programs which allow the students to attend school for part of the day and then work for the other half of the day are in effect in most of our secondary schools.

Chapter Seven

PREVENTING STUDENT DROPOUT

Preventing student dropout is a concern of parents, teachers and all who work with children. Dropout prevention programs have been established to aid efforts to keep students in school.

Children and youth today are often placed in situations where they are given the opportunity to make decisions about their lives which will impact their future life. Many of them do not possess all of the information needed to make the best decision. Reasons often cited for leaving school are pregnancy, family circumstances, economic necessities, substance abuse, lack of academic success and disciplinary action.

I was a teenager during the sixties, and school was sometimes boring. Although some students moved at a slower rate than others, I do not remember anyone in my class, i.e., from first grade through high school graduation, who left school before earning a high school diploma. The possibility of dropping out was never considered because students knew their parents would not consider the notion or allow them to drop out of school. What has changed? It appears as though students today are free to drop out of school. The question is, "Are parents monitoring their children's progress in school?"

I recently encountered a lady who was determined that her son would complete high school. She carefully monitored his progress in school. She acknowledged that he was not the best of students, in fact, she arranged for him to attend a technical school for part of the day. She conveyed to him the importance of completing high school. Mike knew that he would not be able to remain in his mother's home if he dropped out of school. That may appear hard to some, but he recently graduated from high school and is now working.

I am also familiar with a situation in which the individual did not complete high school. The problems first arose when he was 14. Robert stopped showing an interest and began to skip school. He was assigned to various schools in an effort to identify a school which would be agreeable to him. Robert's stepfather often dropped him off at school only to discover that he had sneaked back home. Robert eventually dropped out of school, but continued to remain at home. He did not work, nor did he seek employment. His mother eventually found him a job through someone she knew. Robert was a youngster who was allowed to drop out of school and remain at home. Although he dropped out of school, Robert was not allowed to incur some of the unpleasantries associated with dropping out of school. His parents upheld his decision by not placing any conditions upon his behavior; rather they allowed him to stay home and do nothing.

If a child is old enough to make the decision to drop out of school, then he/she is also old enough to start contributing to his/her support. It's as though youth of today are not asked to accept responsibility for their actions. Robert is now 25 years old and has never finished high school. He still lives with his parents. Youth are often allowed to assume the privileges of an adult, without assuming the responsibilities. Many are not asked to be accountable for their actions.

Dropout Rate

The dropout rate differs in accordance with the definition that is used. National dropout figures hover around 46%, according to the U.S. Office of Education. Those figures are in accord with the perception of the dropout rate as showing the number of students who left school under circumstances that meet the definition of a dropout during a school year as a percentage of the total student population in grades 9–12. McLaughlin (1990) asserted that 81.7% of youth now complete a high school education by age 24. He further asserted that calculations of high national and urban dropout rates based on the number of students who do not graduate by age 18 have resulted in a "phantom crisis."

Is our goal for students to complete their high school education by age 18, or is our goal that students complete their high school education although they may complete it at a later age? Maybe we need to reexamine the issue. The question is emphasized because the answer to the question affects dropout prevention efforts. If our goal is that students ultimately earn a high school diploma before a determined age, our dropout prevention efforts may include pursuing individuals who have left school in an effort to persuade them to return to school as soon as possible.

Palm Beach County, Florida has a program, Project Concern, which involves workers telephoning students who have left school before earning a diploma. In 1989 workers were able to bring back 29% (427 students), of the 1,473 students who dropped out of school the previous year. Of the 427 students who returned, 166 were encouraged to enroll in adult-education classes or work for General Education Diploma certificates, 176 returned to high school, and 18 enrolled in technical education centers. Of the 427 students, 67 were encouraged to enroll in private schools, community colleges or enlist in the armed forces. Many of these students will not earn a diploma before the age of 18, but if they continue in school they will earn a diploma. Programs which target students who have left school in an effort to bring them back to school may be considered dropout prevention programs if we expand our definition of the dropout to include individuals who have left school under circumstances characteristic of the dropout but who may be persuaded to return to school.

Initiation of Dropout Prevention Programs

After researching and comparing dropout prevention programs in six urban areas of the United States, Linden (1990) concluded that a truly effective attendance and dropout prevention program would begin in the elementary school years when patterns of attendance are formed. McLaughlin (1990) postulated that there is no need for costly new state or federal dropout prevention programs because 81.7 percent of youth now complete a high school education by age 24, nearly achieving President George Bush's goal of a 90 percent graduation rate by the year 2000. Reforms are needed that encourage greater parental involvement and give students greater incentives to stay in school.

Importance of Understanding Why Students Leave School

Understanding why students drop out is important in developing effective dropout prevention strategies. Students leave school for many reasons. Pregnancy, family circumstances, economic necessities, substance abuse, lack of academic success, or disciplinary actions can influence a young person's decision to quit school. These reasons should be considered when developing dropout prevention programs. To be effective, a dropout prevention program must respond to the needs of the students.

High Risk Students

The single greatest issue facing American education today is how to improve the education of low achievers and other students at risk of school failure. Efforts are being made to reach children at risk of dropping out of school at earlier ages. Guthrie (1989) identified the following strategies for improving the education of at-risk students:

1. Make at-risk students a priority in the school,
2. Take a comprehensive approach,
3. Invest in staff development,
4. Raise expectations for at-risk students,
5. Provide more quality time for learning,
6. Coordinate instruction for each student,
7. Intervene as early as possible.

Dropout Prevention Strategies

The question often asked is what can be done to prevent student dropout? We can present students with reasons for attending school as soon as they are old enough to question and to understand. We must give students a reason why they should attend school and do their best. This reason must be individualized because students may say, "This is good, but what does it mean to me?" Parents and others must impress upon students the need for an education in order to function in our society. This must begin when the child is in elementary school.

A range of services, beginning in elementary school, should be provided for students. It is important that parents be involved in the education process from their child's first day of attendance at school. Negative attitudes toward school voiced by some students may be related to the lack of parental support for education.

Although efforts should begin in elementary school, junior high school is the critical period for the identification of potential school dropouts. Dropout prevention efforts should be applicable to meet student needs. Student characteristics to consider when planning dropout prevention efforts are: (a) student motivation, (b) adjustment period, (c) pregnancy, and (d) financial hardships.

Dropout prevention strategies should be multiple because there is no single solution to the dropout problem as there is no single reason why students leave school. Reasons students choose to leave school must be considered when planning dropout prevention efforts. The National Dropout Prevention Center, in an effort to determine the most successful approaches to dropout prevention efforts, conducted an analysis in 1990 of current research and practices in more than 350 dropout prevention programs. This resulted in the identification of the following 10 strategies by Duckenfield, et al. (1990) that have had the most positive impact on the dropout rate in communities across the nation.

1. *Parental assistance and involvement.* Parents must be involved in dropout prevention efforts if those efforts are to be successful.

2. *Quality childhood education.* A student's early education experiences will determine the extent and type of educational experiences the student will pursue. Because habits are formed during the early years, it is important that children learn good habits that will benefit them as they progress through school.

3. *Concentrated reading and writing programs.* The ability to read and write is the foundation of success in school. If the basic skills are not learned in the earliest grades students have increasing difficulty with expanding literacy as they progress through the grades. Many students drop out of school because they have not mastered basic reading and writing.

4. *Individualized instruction.* Involves students actively in the learning process by utilizing their interests and aspirations more effectively. Since this progress can capitalize on student's unique learning styles, it allows them to focus upon specific objectives, learn at their own pace and ability level, and be at different points in the curriculum.

5. *Utilization of instructional technologies.* Allows for the individualized and self-paced curriculum which is particularly helpful to at-risk students. The use of computers in teaching traditional subjects has proved attractive to students, especially if the software includes colorful graphics and sound effects.

6. *Mentoring and tutoring.* One-to-one involvement with a significant other, either in a mentoring or tutoring situation, is one of the most effective strategies for helping at-risk students. Peer tutoring and cross age tutoring has been shown to be a particularly powerful intervention for at-risk students.

7. *Summer enhancement programs.* It is estimated that much of the difference in academic achievement between at-risk students and others occurs during the summer. Summer school is now being considered a viable alternative for students at all grade levels. Upward Bound Pro-

grams have also shown tremendous success in working with low income youth.

8. *Flexible schedules and alternative programs.* Alternative schools may be a preventive measure. They have added a humanistic approach to dropout programs. The Part-Time Jobs portion of the Attendance Improvement Dropout Prevention (AIDP) program in New York City provided job-readiness training and job placements in an effort to motivate students to improve academic achievement and school attendance (Mei, Dolores M. et al. 1990).

The Technical Alternative High School was designed to treat an aspect of the dropout problem by offering students a realistic opportunity to experience competence through occupational training integrated with academics and supported by structured counseling activities. The goal of the program was to address the attitudes and behaviors that contribute to the dropout problem by developing a student's sense of competence and worth through meaningful vocational and academic experiences, integrated with social skills training and counseling support (Jambor & Stephen, 1990). Burkham and Lee (1990) noted that transferring from one high school to another may be an important alternative to dropping out.

9. *Staff development program.* Helpful activities include training in identifying at-risk students using special instructional strategies, making shared decisions and developing or enhancing personal characteristics such as empathy and caring.

10. *Community and business collaboration.* School business partnerships, including occupational training, counseling, and prior employment experience, have been effective in reducing the dropout rate in many schools. Work-study programs often involve private industry and non-profit agencies. Burger King opened 10 sites in 1989 to cater to potential dropouts with teachers and staff trained to help them in academics, social problems and job hunting.

An analysis of dropout prevention programs and literature revealed a combination of prevention strategies, including non-punitive approaches, alternative school schedules, and modifying or rescinding policies that tend to discourage at-risk students. The traditional dropout prevention method has been segregation and remediation (Mirochnik, 1990).

Early Intervention

To be most effective a dropout prevention program should be begun in the elementary schools. The author had the experience of working with a potential teenage dropout. After being placed in the local school and after being tested, Dana (not her real name) was placed in a dropout prevention program. She was placed in a smaller size classroom because of the belief that she along with her classmates in the classroom needed to be in a less competitive situation. It was also believed that they needed positive rewards. The class size was limited to 10 students. Although in the fourth grade Dana could not read, she also displayed a total lack of interest in school. The author worked closely with Dana's classroom teacher. The initial goal was to build an interest in school and an interest in learning. Dana stayed in this program for two years. It is my belief that this program saved Dana. She is now in a regular classroom and enjoys and looks forward to school. Dana needed to see how school could work for her. For Dana, school had to be more than a place where she came and sat for a few hours each day. This program helped Dana by helping her to develop a positive attitude towards school as well as showing her that she could have and should expect positive experiences in school. Dropout prevention programs should begin in the elementary grades because that is the time when patterns of school attendance are formed. That is the most opportune time to begin to work with parents and restructure their attitudes towards school as well as the time to get students used to the idea of succeeding in school.

Chapter Eight

WHAT NOW? MAKING SCHOOL APPEALING
TO THE YOUTH OF TODAY

Today's youth are having problems in the school system more than any other period in our history. Our dropout rate is tremendous. Schools are not working for some of our youth. When we turn our heads and choose to focus on those students who seem to do well in our school districts, we deny the existence of the problem. We don't like to talk about the negative side of schooling. Yet when we look at our school system we see many students fail. We see many Johnnys and Bettys becoming dropouts. Until we face up to the fact that Johnny or Betty is a product of our system, we will continue to deny and blame.

Schools blaming parents, parents blaming the school, and the overuse of words such as "lack of motivation" are all approaches which are used to place the student out of reach for helping. What does the youth have to say about the entire problem? Many of them have been quoted as saying that our schools are insensitive, concerned with favoritism, overwhelmed with students and parents, uninteresting, strict, and out of touch. This is quite a list coming from students who are viewed as resistant and potential dropouts. Do schools look at themselves? Most of them do appear to show signs of awareness of a few problems, but many have a blind side or deaf ear to change in major problem areas.

One such problem is teacher burnout. A teacher, for example, is difficult to motivate once he or she has become burned out. For instance, some teachers with twenty-five years of teaching, a master's degree in education, a stubborn attitude, and many frustrations in working with students, are prone not to change their personality, attitude or motivation toward teaching. What multiplies the problem is more than one burned out teacher in a school building. Burned out teachers seem to clique together with negative stories to share about their students.

Unfortunately, some of our students have teachers who care little about whether or not they learn in the classroom. Some teachers' attitudes are that Johnny or Betty should perform in the classroom, control his or her behavior and earn a good grade, and should not be a problem to the teacher. However, when the youth presents a challenge to the teacher in the form of behavior, school performance or attitude, teachers may see this as an opportunity to rid themselves of a child who is "rocking the boat." The point is that teachers enjoy structure, control, silence, obedience, respect and power in the classroom. If a student tries to "buck the system" the consequence is that a teacher will exert his or her authority. Again, some teachers view the classroom as their personal domain and they will use rules and regulations to maintain equilibrium.

The fact is that all youth grow up having a broad range of experiences. Some youth are more active than others, while others may need less structure, and function excellently without guidance. Teachers are not equipped to handle the differences. Moreover, when Johnny brings to the classroom a whole range of unmet needs (Maslow's Hierarchy of Needs), a teacher may not want to get involved with Johnny and his personal problems.

Many of our teachers have negative attitudes because they are underpaid and overworked. Their commitment is short lived when the reality of the school situation sets in. Many teachers are not paid equally to garbage collectors in some cities. This says something about our values in our society. The point is that underpaid teachers who complain about our failing schools don't easily develop a positive attitude toward students who have a broad range of unmet needs.

Problem Administrators

Administrators are sometimes insensitive to teachers, students and parents. Many of them have a deaf ear to student or teacher needs. When teachers are fighting with student crises and daily stresses, some administrators are more concerned with the smooth running of a school building than the actual concerns of teachers. In some cases, teachers are more tuned into what is happening in a school than some school administrators.

I have encountered school principals who have ambitions to climb the administrative ladder and will do anything to achieve their goal. As dictators they control and regulate staff and teachers so that their school can be the top school in the district or city. The media and newsprint are used to visually acknowledge their accomplishments. For example, a newspaper reporter shared a human interest story of one principal's effort to reach into the black community. An illustration: One newspaper reported that Bill Jones, principal of East High School, personally visited black parents to talk with them about their involvement in PTA. When parents visited the school, he always had time to speak with them and share his perceptions of their son's or daughter's progress. He attended a neighborhood church and spoke at several functions in which many parents participated. In addition he was seen in the media discussing his role as a principal and he wrote columns for the local newspaper, addressing issues of today.

In the public eye Bill Jones was seen as a small town hero. He cared about education and people knew it. With this brand of rapport with the public, it was well known that he would eventually reach the school administration or central offices. Bill Jones was determined and goal directed toward obtaining a school administrative position. He did everything that would get him attention. He worked for a higher education administration degree, joined the social clubs, promoted race relations, encouraged individual teachers to win the outstanding award he offered each year, invited the media to his school and stressed academics. Bill wanted his school to be known as an academic school not an athletic school. He wanted his students to do well on scholastic tests so that he could grab some of the glory for their achievement.

Bill Jones strategically plans to forward his own career. Can this be a problem? Yes, when he has deaf ears to people who work with him, parents, students, the community, and his only purpose for being effective is for a promotion, then we have a problem.

Unresponsive Parents

A few years ago I worked with several black parents who seemed to blame the school for everything. They believed the schools were too structured, the teachers were too strict; and the principal was too young and inexperienced. These parents blamed the schools for being overcrowded and unsafe. There were too many young teachers and not enough older and experienced teachers. In other words, the schools were failing to educate their children. The problem here was that these parents had no solutions, but they were absolutely convinced the school system had no solutions either.

Solutions are possible if parents and school officials work together.

The focus should be on the child, not personal agenda. Solutions must include school teachers, parents, and students, and the community.

School Faculty

School teachers have their fears, anger and frustration toward students, administrators, parents and the community. Many of them remember physical attacks or verbal insults. There are a growing number of teachers who are wounded by students and have been provided psychotherapy as a means of learning new coping skills.

Administrators are a source of teacher frustration, especially when administration is perceived by teachers as insensitive to their concerns. In some cases, administrators can be overly structured. This kind of administrator can make a teacher's school life miserable, with policies and regulations that block progress.

Parents and the community may be a problem to the teacher. Parents may sometimes believe the school does not have their interest at heart. Ethnic minority parents often perceive the school as a major problem to the community. For example, a teacher informs African American youngsters that their lips are too big to play a horn in the band. This kind of message can make parents very angry. The school may be seen as a problem to the community.

MAKING SCHOOL APPEALING TO TODAY'S YOUTH

The question is often asked, "How do we make schools appealing to today's youth?" Here are a few recommendations:

1. Use various learning styles in the classroom. Students learn differently.

Some students are usually auditory or experiential, while others may be extraverted or introverted. For example, if a student were introverted and spends much of his or her time alone, forcing these students into a group project with extraverted students might place a damper on a student's motivation. Providing this student with the opportunity to choose between a group and individual projects would give the student a chance to demonstrate his or her maximum ability. Some students operate better individually than with groups. Therefore, a teacher might ask students to choose from either individual or group projects.

2. Have minority representation among teachers and administrators.

Minority representation is important. In the nineties, we are seeing more minorities than ever. By the year 2000, Hispanics are expected to outnumber African Americans and will be the largest group of people of color. It is only fair that minorities are able to see people of color represented in the hierarchy of an organization.

3. Get parents involved in the school.

There are a number of ways to get parents involved with the school system. First, have the principal periodically go into various communities to meet parents. A principal should not wait for problems to occur. He or she should be pro-active and excited about meeting parents of his students. Attend community functions and speak at local churches and civic organizations. Second, get the PTA chapters involved. Send letters and telephone parents to get their reactions to the school system and its current problems. When parents feel they have a sense of ownership in the schools, you will see more involvement. Third, have parents volunteer in the schools. Parents could be security guards, attendance workers and teacher assistants. When parents believe they are involved in their child's education, they will feel more relaxed with the school system.

4. Be creative and develop programs that will utilize the talents of administrators, teachers and parents.

Some innovative programs that incorporate the efforts of administrators, teachers and parents are (a) career day programs, (b) carnivals, (c) parents day, (d) talent shows, and (e) all school picnics.

5. Get the media involved with positive press about the school and its activities.

The media can have a tremendous impact on how a community views their school system. Positive stories give community people a brighter outlook. Share with the press school activities and students accomplishments. Have parents participate in school functions. The six o'clock news, for example, could report on a heart warming story inside the school. Show the positive side of school and help build a positive school image.

6. Provide teachers with staff training in crisis intervention, stress management and student anger control.

Students bring a range of difficult problems into the classroom. Schools are confronted with school violence, excessive drug usage and alcohol. Teachers are in need of specialized training in crises interventions in order to handle some of the problems of students today. For example, students who are angry and out of control can be a potential threat to teachers and peers. A school with negative transactions among students and teachers places everyone under stress. Therefore, teachers and students should be taught stress management.

7. Bring various role models into schools to provide speeches and interaction with students.

Many students identify with successful people. Athletics is one particular area in which young people strive to succeed. Getting a star athlete to speak to students is an excellent way to provide students with positive role models.

8. Reward teachers who reach out to students and improve academic performances.

Good teachers should be rewarded for their extra effort in helping students improve in academic performance. When a teacher reaches out to students who have had academic difficulty in prior classes and provides students with motivation and strategies for change, this person should receive special recognition for going beyond the call of duty. There are strategies for helping students improve such as (a) computer learning, (b) tutors, (c) behavioral learning strategies, and (d) self-esteem building programs.

9. Implement a mentoring program.

Getting young men and women involved with the public schools is a great idea. One way to encourage students to change their negative behavior and become productive members of a community is to invite community members to become mentors. For example, a storeowner may spend one to several hours a week with a youth. This interaction may involve one to one counseling or having good old down home fun together. Through positive association, the youth will learn positive behaviors from his or her mentor and have someone to assist him or her in their drive toward personal goals.

A mentor can share his or her experiences and provide a youth with a sound plan in achieving goals. Often a mentor will listen to personal problems and help the youth arrive at positive solutions.

10. Get industry and business interested in the school so that they will adopt a school.

All over the United States, industry and businesses are beginning to get involved with social problems. No longer are social problems left to social workers, sociologists and urban planners. The private sector has thrown its hat into the arena and they are learning how to deal with social issues. Experts on social issues and major corporations are putting their best minds together to come up with solutions. The Adopt-A-School program is the result of the private sector wanting to get involved with public schools and social problems. These programs are working and succeeding in bridging the gap between the school and the world of work.

Chapter Nine

PULLING IT ALL TOGETHER

One book cannot solve the problems of the dropout, but it may identify and describe issues involving the dropout. This is necessary because we need to know and understand these issues before we seek solutions. *Dropping Out: Issues and Answers* is not an attempt to solve the problem of the dropout. Rather it is an attempt to identify and highlight issues which must be confronted when attempting to alleviate or lower the incidence of high school drop outs, i.e., students who leave school before earning their high school diploma. It should be remembered that there is no one cut-and-dried solution as there is no one prototype which fits the dropout. This ill have served its purpose if it provokes the read xamine the issues surrounding the high vent high school dropouts.

school dropouts are in a dire situation, b them. Entry-level jobs now require skills ar cause of economic conditions, many high scl d to take jobs which at one time would ha h school diplomas. This has pushed the hig out of the job market. The American economy is changing, jobs are scarce. It is difficult, if not impossible, for high school dropouts, if they should happen to find a job, to support themselves or their families on their earnings.

When asked if there is a dropout problem the writers must answer "yes" and ask a thought provoking question: Is the dropout problem merely the fact that people leave school without graduating or is it more? In earlier years this would not have been a problem because these individuals would have been able to locate gainful employment. That is no longer the case, because jobs are no longer readily available for the individual who drops out of school.

Our society is an advanced technological society which requires certain knowledge and skills if the individual is to successfully function within it. A very important skill today and for future generations

85

is computer literacy and skills. Our society has been taken over by the computer, and more and more jobs now require computer skills. These skills may be obtained in high school. The basic skills continue to be necessary for successful functioning in our complex society. Individuals who cannot read nor comprehend what they have read are at a great disadvantage today. Thus the effort to get youths to stay in school and acquire basic skills is of the utmost importance to today's youth.

One aspect of the problem of the dropout is that students are leaving school during a time when the knowledge level is increasing and jobs are scarce. They are leaving school with no marketable skills, unprepared for what lies ahead. The goal is to get them to stay in school and acquire marketable skills.

The individual who leaves school before earning a high school diploma is not aware of what awaits him or her. The stigma of being a dropout and somehow having failed and an inability to find a job await the high school drop out. It is as though he or she wears a "Scarlet Letter" for the whole world to see. Completing high school does not guarantee the individual a job, but it is a necessary first step toward acquiring one.

There may have been an increase in the absolute number of dropouts as there has been an increase in the population, but relatively speaking there has not been an increase in the percentage of dropouts. Percentage wise, there has been a steady decrease in the number of dropouts. In 1920, 16.8% of 17 year olds graduated from high school. In 1940, 50.8% of 17 year olds graduated from high school, but by 1970, 76.5% of 17 year olds graduated from high school.

Students may ask if it is necessary to complete high school. Some think that it isn't, but it most definitely is for their future development. In American society it is imperative for individuals to complete high school because modern American society is highly technological. The completion of high school prepares them to function within that society.

After reflecting upon their high school experiences some readers may ask, "What does the individual gain from his or her high school experiences?" Upon the completion of high school, the student should have received a broad overview of the larger society and how it operates and should have a basic understanding of its laws and institutions. Hopefully, they will have acquired the necessary skills and knowledge necessary to function in the larger society.

Our educational system has changed and continues to change. Some have called for more changes in our educational system in order that it may reflect the world in which the individual lives. One change in our educational system which had far reaching effects upon all aspects of education was the integration of our schools. Another was the inclusion of handicapped students into the mainstream of the educational curriculum and activities. These changes have made our educational system and classes more heterogeneous. They have also increased the number and types of students in our educational system. The emphasis upon women being treated equally has affected the classes being offered to both men and women.

Schools are the primary tools of socialization in our society and are used in preparing the individual to assume a responsible position within society. In our present society if schools were not used as tools of socialization then what would be used? More often than not, both parents are busy working. Who is available to teach the individual all he or she will need to know to survive in the larger society? There is so much that an individual needs to know, hence the importance of formal education. Knowledge has increased, and continues to increase at a much faster rate than at any other period in our history.

Most individuals, when looking back on their school experiences, will say that much of what they learned in school is or was not relevant to their life experiences. The question is, what can be done to make school more relevant? A number of things can be done. Reading materials that our students are exposed to in the schools should be regularly updated to reflect the changing world in which our youth live. They should address everyday issues rather than classical literature. Math classes should be taught in a manner which allows the student to apply concepts to everyday problems. What is wrong with teaching students how to balance a checkbook? In other words, let's teach children about life in the 1990s and how to function in the 1990's. Our curriculum needs to be updated. Let's provide more challenging and stimulating experiences for our youth. Let's provide them opportunities to visit plants, etc., or other situations, so they will get an understanding of how the real world operates. These opportunities are often provided problem students in an effort to motivate them. These opportunities should be provided for all students. Many students graduate from high school with no idea of what it takes to survive in the real world. What about introducing them to varied occupations n our social studies classes, beginning in late elementary school? In other words, let's now begin to prepare our students for what lies ahead upon their graduation. Let's challenge them to think about and prepare for what lies ahead.

REFERENCES

Alexander, K., Natriello, G., and Pallas, A.M.: *For whom the school bell tolls — the impact of dropping out on cognitive performance,* Report #356 National Institute of Education (Eds.), Washington, DC, 1985.

Alpert, Geoffrey and Dunhamm, Roger: Keeping academically marginal youth in school, *Youth and Society, 17:*345–361, 1986.

Beck, Robert Holmes: *A social history of education — foundations of education series,* Englewood Cliffs, Prentice-Hall, 1965.

Benedict, R. R., Snell, R. and Miller, D.: Enterprise high — helping school dropouts become self-supporting adults, *Educational Leadership,* 3:87.

Boyer, Richard and Savagean, David: *The places rated almanac,* Englewood Cliffs, Prentice-Hall, 1989.

Burkham, David T. and Lee, Valerie E.: *Changing high school — an alternative to dropping out,* Annual Meeting of the American Educational Research Association, Boston, 1990, ED323646.

Collins, Randall: *The credential society — an historical sociology of education and stratification,* New York, Academic Press, 1979.

Cueller, Alfredo and Culler, Mariano-Florentino: *From dropout to high achiever — an understanding of academic excellence through an analysis of dropouts and students at risk,* San Diego, San Diego State Univ., 1990, ED322252.

Dropout Prevention — twelve successful strategies to consider in a comprehensive dropout prevention program. Clemson, National Dropout Prevention Center, 1990, ED322461.

Duckenfield, Marty, et al.: *Effective strategies for far west laboratory for educational research and development — strategies for dropout prevention,* San Francisco, 1989, ED318833.

Far West Laboratory for Educational Research and Development: *Strategies for dropout prevention,* San Francisco, 1989, ED 318833.

Goodman, Paul: The universal trap. In Schreiber, Daniel, (Ed.): *The school dropout,* Washington, DC, NASW, 1964.

Guthrie, Larry F.: *What schools can do for students at risk,* San Francisco, Far West laboratory for Educational Research and Development, 1989, ED323276.

Gutek, Gerald.: *Education and schooling in America,* Englewood Cliffs, Prentice-Hall, 1988.

Historical Statistics of the United States: Washington, DC, U.S. Governmental Printing Office.

Jambor, Stephen O.: *The technical alternative high school — a federal demonstration pro-*

gram using comprehensive programming to support drop out prevention, Nashville, National Dropout Prevention Conference, 1990, Ed323442.

Justiz, M. J. and Kameen, M. C.: Business offers a hand to education, *Phi Delta Kappan,* 1:87.

Kentucky Governor's Council on Vocational Education: *The role of vocational education in dropout prevention,* Frankfort, 1989, ED319940.

Maslow, A. H. *Toward a Psychology of Being* (2nd ed.). New York. Van Nostrand Reinhold, 1968.

McLaughlin, Michael J.: High school dropouts—how much of a crisis? *Backgrounder,* 781, Washington, DC, Heritage Foundation, 1990, ED325582.

Mei, Dolores M. et al.: *A.I.D.P. part time jobs 1988–89—OREA report,* Brooklyn, New York City Board of Education, Office of Research and Evaluation and Assessment, 1990, ED323308.

Merchant, Betty: *Dropping out—a preschool through high school concern,* Berkeley, Policy Analysis for California Education, 1987, ED320293.

Mirochnik, Denise and McCaul, Edward J.: *Public school dropouts—a contextual approach,* Orono, Occasional Paper Series, No. 5, Maine University, Penquis Superintendents Association Research Cooperative, 1990, ED324152.

Official Florida Statutes, Section 228.04(29) p. 1434. State of Florida, Tallahassee, 1987.

National Committee on Excellence in Education: *A nation at risk,* Washington, DC, 1983.

NCTM standards emphasize application of math skills: *Education USA,* 31:30, 1989.

Ogletree, Earl J.: *Alternative schools and dropout rate,* Chicago, Chicago State University, Department of Curriculum and Instruction, 60628-1598ED, 324382.

Pellicano, R. R.: At risk—a view of social advantage, *Educational Leadership,* 3:87.

Schreiber, Daniel.: *The school dropout,* Washington, DC, National Education Association, 1964.

Smink, Jay.: *Mentoring programs for at-risk youth—dropout prevention research report,* Clemson, National Dropout Prevention Center, February 1990, ED318931.

Smith, Judith.: *Voices of exile—the public school from the dropout's perspective,* Masters of Education Special Education Project, Mansfield, 1986, pp. 1–41.

Statistical Abstract of the United States. 1966, 1971, 1976, Washington, DC, U.S. Government Printing Office.

Wehhlage, Gary and Rutter, Robert A.: *Dropping out—how much do schools contribute to the problem?* Wisconsin Center for Educational Research, Madison, 1985, pp. 1–55, ED 275799.

INDEX

A

A Nation At Risk and educational reform, 56–57

African Americans, racial segregation and, 64

Alexander, K., 48, 89

Alpert, Geoffrey, 89

Alternative schools, 11

American Women, 1964 Civil Rights Act and, 65

At-risk children and youths (*see also* Potential dropouts identification)
    methods of assessing, 19

B

Beck, Robert Holmes, 34, 61, 62, 69, 89

Benedict, R. R., 53, 55, 89

Boyer, Richard, 39, 89

Brown vs. Board of Education of Topeka, 64

Burkham, David T., 74, 89

C

Campus Compact, 11

Child labor
    changes in, 62–63
    current minimum age, 62

Cities in School program, 10–11

Civil Rights Act of 1964, 65

Collins, Randall, 48, 54, 89

Compulsory school attendance, 60–61
    contents of law, 61
    first state to pass, 61
    number high school graduates, 62
    purpose of, 61

Computer literacy and skills, importance of, 50–51, 60, 85–86

Crime, relationship school attendance to increase in, 5

Cueller, Alfredo, 89

Culler, Mariano-Florentino, 89

Curriculum relevance, 50–54
    business and economic courses, 52
    career days, 53–54
    clerical skills, 51
    computer classes, 50–51, 60, 85–86
    effects of economic slowdown, 54
    family life courses, 52
    math skills, 53
    need to make classes more relevant, 87–88
    survival courses, 53
    teaching from life, 52
    word processor skills, 51

D

Diploma, high school
    history of, 31, 45
    importance of, 3, 32, 45
    increased value of, 63

Dropout
    alternative schools for, 11
    Burger King Academics, 11, 74
    decrease in percentage of, 86
    decrease in relative number of, 61
    definition of, 3, 59
    employment following, 46
    factors concerning, 49–50
    goal of programs, 86
    incidence of, 3, 86
    lack jobs for, 46, 85
    negative consequences of, 3–6
    negative view of, 59
    potential (*see* Potential dropout identification)
    predictors of, 5